Hunting Big Bears

Brown, Grizzly & Polar Bears

Hunting Wisdom Library

MINNETONKA, MINNESOTA

About the Author

As the son of a trapper, J. Wayne Fears grew up hunting. After college he worked as a professional wildlife manager and hunting outfitter. For more than three decades he has been one of America's most prolific hunting writers with more than 3,000 magazine articles and 14 books to his credit. Currently he is the editor of *Rural Sportsman* magazine, a national magazine on wildlife management for farmers and ranchers. His fascination with big bears began with his first grizzly hunt, on which he took a bear with one shot. His next grizzly took five shots and almost got into his hip pocket.

"To Brooke, Brandi and Justin. May there be huntable populations of big bears when your time comes."

HUNTING BIG BEARS
Brown, Grizzly & Polar Bears

Mike Vail
Vice President, Product and Business Development

Tom Carpenter
Director of Book Development

Dan Kennedy
Book Production Manager
Photo Editor

Heather Koshiol
Book Development Coordinator

Shari Gross
Book Development Assistant

Colorbrite Inc.
Design and Production

Phil Aarrestad
Commissioned Photography

Special Thanks to Cabin Fever Sporting Goods, Victoria, MN

PHOTO CREDITS

Cover photo: Alberta Grizzly Bear by Donald M. Jones.
Other photography: Phil Aarrestad: 48, 53, 58, 60 (both), 67, 70, 71 (top), 72 (bottom), 77, 78, 79, 80, 84–85 (both), 102, 137, 143, 146; Kenny Bahr: 14 (bottom), 17, 18 (bottom), 23 (top), 24, 33 (top); Bill Buckley/The Green Agency: 98; Tom Carpenter/NAHC: 72 (top); Tim Christie: 4, 12, 25, 27, 28 (top), 36–37, 38, 41 (top), 46, 86, 89, 94, 110–111, 112, 114, 115, 117 (top), 122, 127, 128–129, 131, 138, 136–137, 149, 150–151; Judd Cooney: 28 (bottom), 51, 66, 130, 145; Jeanne Drake: 18 (top), 22, 26–27, 31, 154; Michael Francis: 11, 16, 18 (middle), 125, 30 (bottom), 32, 43 (bottom), 87, 117 (bottom), 125, 134, 139 (bottom); Donald Jones: Cover, 1, 19, 30 (top), 42 (top), 69, 75, 82, 104–105, 111, 116, 119, 148–149, 152; Lee Kline: 9 (bottom), 10, 29, 40 (top), 40 (bottom), 42 (bottom), 43 (top), 153; Neal Mishler: 150; Jim Shockey: 35, 49, 52–53, 55, 63, 74, 76–77, 107, 108; Dusan Smetana: 15, 33 (bottom), 39, 50, 54–55, 62 (bottom), 71 (bottom), 80–81, 88, 132, 133; Ron Spomer: 7, 9 (top), 13, 14 (top), 23 (bottom), 34–35, 41 (bottom), 56, 57, 61, 62 (top), 91, 99, 113, 118, 120, 121, 129, 135, 139, 144; Bryce Towsley: 90, 93; Larry Weishun: 100, 101, 103. Remaining photographs property of NAHC: 47, 68, 83 (both), 97, 109.
Artwork & Illustrations: Virgil Beck: 6; David Rottinghaus: 140 (top).

The Boone and Crockett Club's score chart is reproduced on page 141 courtesy of the Boone and Crockett Club, 250 Station Dr., Missoula, MT 59801, 406/542-1888, www.boone-crockett.org. The Boone and Crockett Club logo is a Registered Trademark reproduced with express written permission of the Boone and Crockett Club.

The Pope & Young Club's scoring form on page 141 is printed with permission of Pope & Young Club, P.O. Box 548, Chatfield, MN 55923, 507/867-4144, www.pope-young.org.

1 2 3 4 5 6 7 8 / 03 02 01 00

ISBN 1-58159-122-5

North American Hunting Club
12301 Whitewater Drive
Minnetonka, MN 55343
www.huntingclub.com

Table of Contents

Foreword

*I*f you've ever been there, you know the feeling. I still can't get used to it.

There was that time on a British Columbia hunt when an honest-to-goodness 7-foot boar towered over me at 13 steps. With my bow in hand and no good shot, my heart throttled my chest at 120 bpm (beats per minute) until the bear turned and lumbered into the forest.

There was that time when we were elk hunting in Wyoming, cow-calling late one afternoon during a light October snowfall. My guide caught movement and hissed, "Bear!" Sure enough, a silver-tipped griz had stalked silently to within 40 yards of our position, probably looking for an elk dinner. When we stood, the bear bolted. Other elk hunters haven't been so lucky.

There was that time on Kodiak Island, Alaska, hunting for Sitka black-tailed deer. Late in the afternoon we glassed back toward our tents a mile away and spotted a giant 9-foot Alaska brown bear feeding along the lakeshore. He was only a

few hundred yards from our food and shelter. So my two hunting companions and I hustled toward him hoping to frighten him out of "our" valley. The bear left, but he took his time. And he looked over his shoulder a couple times as if to say, "I'll be back." I slept poorly that night and every night the rest of the trip.

Bears, especially the "Big Three"—Alaska brown bears, grizzlies and polar bears—can easily be called the ultimate that North American hunting has to offer. They are cunning. They are immeasurably powerful. They prosper at the most remote reaches of wilderness this continent offers. And they can turn the tables and hunt *you*. All of this makes for adventure difficult to put to words.

This book does an excellent job, though, of capturing the essence of "Hunting Big Bears." If you dare imagine what it might be like, or dream of someday hunting these creatures for yourself, you must read this book. And you should read it even if you might never plan to walk where the big bears do. Why? So that you can feel an electrifying adrenaline surge and heart-hammering rush like you've never felt before. Come along; you'll see what I mean.

Gregg

Gregg Gutschow
Executive Director, North American Hunting Club

DANGEROUS GAME, DANGEROUS HUNTING

Harvey Cardinal was more than an average hunter. He was a Native American who had spent his life trapping and hunting and guiding hunters in northeastern British Columbia. Having grown up in grizzly country, he knew that big bears are unpredictable and smart.

HARVEY CARDINAL'S STORY

Nighttime temperatures were as low as minus 30°F that fateful day. Harvey Cardinal had left his home near Fort St. John to visit some friends who were trapping along the Doig River in British Columbia.

Cardinal arrived at his friends' cabin amid a lot of excitement: The trappers had come across fresh tracks of a large grizzly that morning as they ran their trapline. It wasn't unusual to see a grizzly, but it was odd that the bear was not hibernating during this midwinter, bitter cold. Cardinal couldn't resist thinking about the money he could get for a grizzly pelt with a winter coat. At daybreak he left the cabin with his rifle to hunt the bear alone.

As he set out across the snow-covered ground, he probably gave some thought to how dangerous a grizzly can be. There had been, over the years, three grizzly attacks in that area. Two attacks involved hunting guides—one who jumped off a cliff to save his life and another who was charged by a wounded bear he was trailing for a hunter. The third victim was a hunter who was mauled when he walked up on a moose kill that a grizzly had claimed.

Cardinal reached the bear tracks the trappers had found and started following them. As he stayed on the trail, the tracks became fresher, and with his experience, he must have known that he was getting close to the bear. Then, without warning, a massive paw struck the side of Cardinal's head from behind, shattering his skull. The bear had evidently hidden and allowed Cardinal to walk by so that it could attack from the rear. Its attack was obviously without warning: Cardinal's mittens were still on his hands; his rifle's safety was still on.

When Cardinal didn't return, a search party was organized early the next morning. They soon found a horrifying sight. Much of Cardinal's upper body had been eaten by the bear.

Welcome to the exciting world of big bear hunting! It is a world full of adventure where mistakes can be deadly.

EXCITING & UNPREDICTABLE

Most big game hunters name the grizzly, brown or polar bear as the North American game animal they would most like to hunt. Those who have never hunted big bears often yearn to because of magazine articles they've read describing the close calls encountered when hunting these animals. Another reason many hunters want to take a big bear: One makes a massive and impressive trophy.

For those who have hunted these giant carnivores, the reasons for feeling compelled to chase them is far deeper than what is found in a magazine story or a rug. It is the respect and admiration for a creature that almost defies description. What you can say about one bear doesn't apply to another bear. What a bear will do today, he won't do tomorrow. When you think he's dumb, he will make you a fool. In short, bears are the most unpredictable animals we hunt in North America.

When you add to that the fact that they are intelligent, vindictive, courageous, cunning, stubborn,

It is the danger associated with hunting big bears that gets much attention from hunters, and perhaps rightfully so.

shy, tenacious, strong, dangerous (and found in some of the most beautiful yet harsh country in the world) you have everything a hunter could want in a trophy animal.

DANGEROUS HUNTING

More than anything, the danger associated with big bear hunting gets more attention from hunters, and perhaps rightfully so. Under the right conditions, bears will hunt you just as hard as you hunt them.

As I researched this book, I tried to determine a reasonably accurate number of bear attacks during the past 50 years by polar, grizzly and brown bears. I learned that this is not possible: There is no single record-keeping source for such incidents, and there have undoubtedly been many unrecorded maulings and close calls.

A sow with cubs is as potentially dangerous as any animal found in North America. She is willing to give a good fight and even her life to defend her offspring.

One Mean Grizzly

Almost everyone who guides or outfits hunters for these big bears has had some close calls. Guy Anttila of Taku Safari, Inc., a guiding service in British Columbia, told me about the most aggressive behavior he had ever seen displayed by a grizzly. One October, he and his wife were photographing grizzlies that were trying to catch salmon on the Taku River. On their second day of filming, they recorded some good footage of several grizzlies and were now concentrating their efforts on a sow with a three-year-old cub still traveling with her.

After an hour of chasing and eating salmon, the sow and cub crossed over to the side of the river where the Anttilas were hidden in some driftwood. Unaware of the humans' presence, the sow and cub walked into the willows and alders some 80 yards away. The Anttilas knew the sow would soon pick up their scent, because the wind was blowing toward her.

Guy assumed the sow and cub would leave the area once they picked up their scent. With their rifle leaning against the drift logs, the Anttilas discussed their photography. That's when things got interesting. Luckily, Guy was facing the right direction to see the big sow break out of the willows at a distance of 45 yards. She was coming on the run, up the scent trail, her head down in a silent charge. Sand was flying behind every step.

Anttila shouted at the bear as he reached for the rifle, but this just gave the bear a better fix on their location. The next thing Anttila knew, the open sights on his .375 H&H Mag. were centered on the bear. He instinctively shifted the aim slightly to the right to miss the face as he fired. The bullet hit the sow in the left shoulder, stopping her. It took a second shot through the shoulder to kill her.

An Unwanted Visitor

A similar charge happened to a guide in British Columbia. North American Hunting Club Life Member Igor Steciw was guiding a hunter for moose and black bears. It was October, and the day had been cloudy with intermittent rain. Late in the afternoon, the weather cleared and Steciw thought it would be a good time to sit on a hillside and do some glassing. They were near a small, unnamed lake at the upper drainage of the Skeena River, and the coho salmon were at the height of their spawning run.

After only 15 minutes on the hillside, the two men heard the loud crack of a branch breaking, then another. When they looked toward the sound, they saw a large grizzly walking the shoreline of the lake about 300 yards away.

Since the hunter didn't have a grizzly tag, they took pictures of the bear as he ambled in their direction. In the last frame Steciw took, the bear was about 25 yards away and heard the camera shutter click. That got the bear excited. It barked a few times and stood on its hind legs. Steciw called out to the bear, "Go on home, boy," expecting it to take off in a run. But the bear grunted, went back down on all fours, and stood up again.

Again Igor yelled, "Go on, get out of here." To the men's amazement, the bear now went down on all fours and charged at full speed, taking big leaps toward the hunters. Steciw's rifle went up to his shoulder in a flash, and he fired once, twice and a third time. The third shot turned back the charge. The bear was now sideways at about 20 feet. At this point, Steciw took aim behind the left shoulder and fired. The bear wavered through a few steps, went down and rolled off the hill. All was quiet again. The bear squared 7 feet 11 inches and was dark brown with silver tips from forehead to tail.

Big bears like to stand up to get a better view of a suspicious noise or scent.

A Not-So-Cuddly Polar Bear

The unpredictable nature of large bears keeps a hunter on his toes all the time, whether he is in the field hunting or in camp resting.

A good example of this was related to me by Jerome Knap of Canada North Outfitting, a polar bear guiding service. One of Jerome's hunters and an Eskimo guide were polar bear hunting at the northern end of Baffin Island at the mouth of Admiralty Inlet. During the first two days of the hunt, the hunter saw nine bears, including two males in the nine-foot class. Hunters don't normally pass up nine-foot bears, but in this case, the hunter did so because he and his guides had found some day-old tracks of a bear that would go over 11 feet. They decided to hold out for that bear.

On the third morning, the hunters were still asleep in an igloo when the chained dogs started to bark. One of the guides, thinking another dog team was approaching, crawled out of the igloo to see what was happening. There, just 15 yards from the igloo, was a nine-foot polar bear eating on the carcass of a seal that had been shot the day before for food. The guide retreated into the igloo and told the hunter.

Thinking it a good opportunity to photograph a polar bear, the hunter used his knife to chip a hole in the side of the igloo large enough to stick his camera lens through. As he started to take a picture, the bear looked up and saw the black spot on the side of the igloo. It charged instantly. The igloo half collapsed under the bear's attack. Then, backing away, the bear spotted the men. As the bruin charged again, the hunter grabbed his rifle and shot, killing the bear two paces away.

Polar bears have been known to consider hunters a food item, along with seals and other mammals.

A Tailgating Brown Bear

While the brown and grizzly bears seem to dislike the scent of man, there are occasions when it doesn't seem to matter.

One fall I was hunting caribou on the Alaska Peninsula in an area of low-rolling tundra hills scattered with small lakes. There was little vegetation in the area, and long stalks were required to get near the caribou bulls found moving through the area. Walking across the wet tussocks was tough and time-consuming.

Early one morning I spotted two large bulls about three miles from my small spike camp and set out to try for the larger of the two. By the time I got to where the bulls had been, they had moved on, putting too much distance between us to cover that day. Disappointed, I started the long walk back to camp.

As I topped the first hill on my return trip, I looked back to see a large brown bear following me some 400 yards back. He was a beautiful animal with long hair waving in the stiff breeze that blew from me to him. I didn't have a bear tag, so I just sat down to admire him and see what his plans were.

With the wind blowing toward him, he must have scented me, but it didn't seem to have any effect. When I sat down, he lay down. I waited and he waited. When I got up, he got up. Once again I headed back toward camp, now looking back more than ahead. When I would go down into a low area and couldn't see him, I would always be ready as I approached the top of the next hill, half expecting him to be in front of me.

But, he never closed the distance, and he basically did whatever I did. When I reached camp, he disappeared just as quickly as he had appeared, and I never saw him again—not because I wasn't looking, though!

A Polar Bear in Camp

Most big bears are naturally shy, and if given the chance would prefer to avoid a confrontation with people. But the polar bear doesn't see it that way. In fact, he has the reputation of being the only animal in the world that will instinctively stalk and kill a person.

Jerome Knap points out that a polar bear doesn't have to be wounded to be dangerous, nor does it have to be disturbed or angered or have its young threatened. All you have to do is be in its kingdom of ice and snow. You are flesh, blood and bones, and thereby edible.

Knap tells me that every year, a dozen or more polar bears are killed in the Canadian Arctic because they attacked or were about to attack people. Polar bears stalk people whenever they are hungry, and polar bears are hungry most of the time. A number of Knap's hunters have filled their tags in camp. As Knap explains, "Some of these hunters were not even fully dressed when the bear was shot. At first glance, this seems to be a rather anticlimactic way to shoot a polar bear, until you remember that the bear came to camp to feed on whatever was available, including the hunter!"

This view of a polar bear in the wild is enough to make the hair on the back of any hunter's neck stand up.

A big bear's will to live is unmatched by any other North American species. It can take a lot of lead to put a big bear down for good. These animals define the terms big, strong, tough, muscular.

TOUGH TO KILL

Another fact about big bears that makes them special to the big game hunter is their tenacity. These animals' desire to keep on living is unmatched by any other animal. Not only that, but they are built to take a lot of punishment and stay on their feet.

As will be demonstrated throughout this book, grizzly, brown and polar bears can take a lot of lead from hunters. If a bear is not anchored with broken shoulders, he can "get in your hip pocket" in a hurry or make it into the brush, which assures you of much more excitement—more excitement than many hunters are ready for!

A Will to Live

I have seen a grizzly hit through the lungs stay on his feet and go for 2 1/2 miles, leaving not a drop of blood for the first one-half mile, before he dropped

dead. That was an exciting trailing job.

I once spent the night in a remote Indian village where one of the elder members invited me to his house to look at a huge grizzly rug he had. That rug had 21 holes in it where the bear had been hit. The old man told me that he and his family had ambushed the bear at the bottom of a cliff. Standing on the top of the cliff, they shot until the bear went down. The Indians were almost out of ammo when the bear finally fell.

Jerome Knap tells of one of his hunters who had a close call with a wounded polar bear because the scope mounts on the hunter's rifle had jarred loose. As a result, the rifle was shooting a foot to the left at 100 yards. Before the hunter discovered this problem, he got an opportunity to take a big bear. He emptied his rifle at the bear, hitting it each time, but never with a shot that would break him down. The guide finally dropped the bear four feet from them. The bear had taken seven hits before he went down.

Introduction

Blood Trail Excitement

The Far North has many stories of bears that took several solid hits, yet managed to hunt the hunters or to ambush them.

I was on a blood trail with three other hunters following a mountain grizzly that had taken three shots in the upper part of the body. There was little blood to follow, and the grizzly had run into a wide creekbed covered with willows that stood about head high to a man.

One of the banks of the creek was about 10 feet tall, and a hunter walking on it could see down into some of the willows. The other bank was low and almost 100 yards away, offering no help. A hunter from Minnesota climbed up on the high bank, and the other three of us, walking abreast about eight feet apart, began to pick our way through the tangle of willows. The bear had been in the willows for more than an hour, and we all hoped he was now dead. It was unusually warm as we ever-so-slowly moved a few feet, stopping often to listen for any sign of life up ahead.

It is always an uncomfortable feeling to follow a hit bear, and in the thick willows with insects swarming all around my head, it was almost smothering. I came to a ditch-like depression that I had to climb into, and as I slid down the bank, my .30-06 felt more like an air rifle. I peeked over the opposite bank before I climbed up and thought to myself, "How do I get myself into these situations?"

Moving back into the willows, I whistled to let the other two hunters know it was me. When I did, a brown mass exploded right in front of me. "God, it's 10 feet tall!" I thought, as I swung my rifle up.

"Damn, it's running over me!" I heard the hunter just to my left cry.

The crashing of the willows was deafening, and this was all going on within a few feet of me. I couldn't identify enough of the creature to get a sight picture. My mind raced as I moved the rifle around. "You're in trouble, Fears, if you don't put this bear down fast," I told myself. Then on top of the brown mass I saw the white antlers of a bull moose. He had been bedded down in a small opening in the willows and was so confused with the three of us being in the willows with him that he almost ran over two of us. Why one of us didn't shoot him, I'll never know.

Soon after the moose scare was over, the hunter on the high bank shouted. He had spotted the bear dead at the bottom of the bank. I don't think I have ever been more glad to have a trailing session over. The moose had about sapped all the courage out of us.

Following a hit bear into the brush is uncomfortable. Having a brown mass explode right in front of your eyes is terrifying. Are you ready?

A SPECIAL KIND OF HUNTING

No other hunt in North America can give you the thrill of a big bear hunt. Aside from the bears themselves, other things associated with bear hunting make it special. The hunt can include a long, leisurely morning spent sitting against a warm, sun-bathed rock using binoculars to cover every inch of a vast valley or opposite mountain slope. When a bear is spotted, it may suddenly mean a three-mile hike over boggy ground, through alder jungles and across cold, rushing streams. It may incorporate a climb up a slope that's so steep you wonder if you can get up it. This is typical of inland grizzly hunting.

On early spring hunts, you may be on snowshoes doing the same things. Most of the guides I've worked and hunted with will confirm this: Your chance of success on grizzlies is directly related to the physical shape you are in. The country is vast and rough, and bear are scattered. Cross-country travel on foot is a major part of the hunt.

Brown bear hunting can be different. I have hunted along the coast of British Columbia with guide Cy Ford, with the day divided between hours of cruising waterways in a large flatbottom boat, sitting and watching tidal flats, and walking in hip boots through thick brush to get to openings along the creeks in that area. The air was often thundering with the sound of snow slides as the spring thaw occurred. Our camp was a small cabin cruiser, and we were ever mindful of the drastic changes in the tide.

A BEAR IN THE BOAT?

Other brown bear hunts may involve floating small rivers and creeks with an inflatable boat. One of the best stories I've heard that describes how exciting this type of hunting can be is told by my friend Bob Good. Good was hunting brown bears with guide Ken Fanning along a small creek near Yakutat, Alaska. Here is the story in Good's words:

"We were floating a small side stream of the Situk

Most big bear hunting involves long periods of carefully glassing a vast amount of beautiful country.

River when we came to a narrow cut barely wide enough to float the raft. The banks were about three feet high over us, and covered with a mix of alder stands and bear grass. We had just got started into the cut when an underwater branch snagged the bottom of the raft, like a clock pendulum banging

Many grizzly hunts are conducted along rivers and tidal flats where a boat is used for transportation and scouting.

against tangles of roots on either side. I turned to look at Ken just in time to see his jaw hit his chest. In brown bear country, you don't have to ask what has caused your partner's sudden start."

"Spinning back around, I snatched my Contender from its holster and looked up. An eight-foot brown bear boar was standing directly over us, trying to understand what in the world had disturbed his stream-side nap. We were so close that I'm sure in his limited eyesight he was looking at the whole bobbing unit of raft and hunters as some two-headed monster about the size of an elephant that was gurgling an endless spray of white foam."

"He looked upset, but confused. This was not a bear we wanted to shoot. Number one, he wasn't quite trophy size, and number two, with one easy jump, even fatally wounded, he could land in our stuck craft faster than two panicked hunters could ever execute a satisfactory abandon-ship drill. It was a standoff."

"Behind me, I heard the safety catch on Ken's .458 click ahead. I'd never been able to hear it before. At the moment, it seemed ominously loud. Ken was now talking

in loud expletives to the bear, advising him it was in his best interest to vacate the area. The bear dropped to all fours, took two steps forward and reared erect again, this time popping his teeth rapidly—a bad sign. Only then did we notice the recently ripped hide and dried blood on his face.

"This guy was apparently resting after a fight when we came merrily along and banged into his bedside. He was going to be long on anger and short on caution. It was not a good situation. 'Tense' doesn't quite describe it."

"At the bear's feet was a broken branch."

" 'Bob, if that son-of-a-b—h steps over that branch, unload on him with everything you've got, and don't stop shooting until you are empty!' Ken instructed."

"By now, I had the Contender zeroed on the bear's chest and a .44 Redhawk balanced in my lap for a quick grab. I had already decided that the broken branch was the demarcation line even before Ken spoke. The bear continued to stare at us with that piggish look bears have that sends a chill right through you. His jaws continued to snap and pop. The air was tense with electricity. As the raft swung

During the salmon run, the dinner bell rings for bears. Hunting along salmon streams at that time can be very productive.

and bobbed with the current, I tried to stay calm and keep the crosshairs pointed somewhere near the bear's brisket; neither was easy.

"With a 'woof,' the bear suddenly whirled and was gone, the swishing alders marking his retreat. Neither Ken nor I moved until we were certain the irritated bear was indeed gone."

"Slowly we returned the guns to rest position and looked at each other with sheepish grins. After unsnagging our raft, we floated on, trying to offset the seriousness of the previous predicament with a nervous chuckle, but we were unusually tense the rest of the day. That bear had been just too close."

"Two years later, Ken's very capable assistant guide, Pierce Nelson, and I killed a bear within 200 yards of that same cut."

Some brown bear hunting during the fall is done by watching streams filled with salmon. This might mean a 10-minute walk from a spike camp or a two-hour walk thorough boggy alders from a base camp. Other hunts may be from a boat glassing sandy beaches. Once the bear is spotted, a long and sometimes interesting stalk through dark timber may be in store before you can get into a good shooting position.

Polar Bear Adventures

The polar bear hunt of today is done only one way: the traditional Eskimo hunt with dog team. It is a most demanding hunt, both physically and mentally. It involves going out on the polar ice, living there in igloos or tents with Eskimo guides and meeting the polar bear on his own terms.

Techniques vary from sitting on high icebergs and using binoculars for hours, to finding fresh tracks and staying with them for three or four days and camping right on the tracks at night.

The hunter will find the wind and temperatures bitter and the camps less than plush. The paying hunter will be expected to help his guides with camp chores. This hunt tests both the hunter and his equipment.

A Different Kind of Fun

The weather that goes with bear hunting helps make it special and has been known to cause many hunters to stop their hunt early to retreat to the comforts of the modern world. Obviously, below-zero temperatures, wind and snow are typical in polar bear country. Grizzly and brown bear weather varies depending upon whether it is a spring or fall hunt and where you are hunting.

I normally think of bear hunting weather as being cold with wind-blown rain and some snow. I have seen hunts that were in deep snow with more snow falling off and on for the entire hunt. I have hunted on days with a mixture of temperatures high enough to bring out the insects by day, and low enough to produce a light snowfall at night. I have had a spike camp blown away and others so wet there wasn't a dry place to sleep. I have been snowed in at a spike camp until the food almost ran out.

Bad weather is usually associated with hunts for grizzlies and polar bears. It's all part of the adventure of the hunt.

You know what? I loved every one of those camps.

While I have been on some relatively easy bear hunts, most were hard work with long hours spent in rough weather conditions, but that's part of what makes bear hunting special. Not everyone is cut out to hunt big bears. If you are, or if you dream of it, hang on. This book is for you!

If your idea of fun is sitting on a gas can under a dripping tarp, eating soggy freeze-dried food after walking eight miles in a downpour, knowing that your wet sleeping bag is waiting for you and that tomorrow morning you will again try to get within 50 yards of one of the smartest, most dangerous animals on earth, then welcome to the world of big bear hunting.

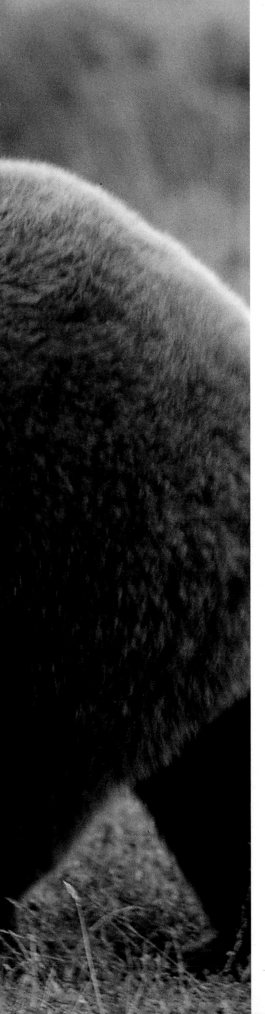

Chapter One

UNDERSTANDING BIG BEARS

When you think about the foundation of successful hunting, going after big bears is the same as any other kind of hunting: You have to understand the animal you are pursuing. Here's what you need to know about brown, grizzly and polar bears to find them in their habitats and to hunt them effectively. Beyond that, these are just plain fascinating animals to know more about.

Polar Bear

Grizzly Bear

Brown Bear

BIG BEAR HISTORY

According to scientists, giant bears existed in North America more than one million years ago, but only their fossil remains could be found when bears as we know them first arrived. The grizzly bear probably came from Asia during the Ice Age, over the Bering Strait land bridge. The polar bear came along later and evolved from the brown bear of northern Russia.

North America's big bears are two of eight species of bear, which are found in 90 countries around the world. The other bears are the black bear of North America, speckled bear of South America, Asiatic black bear found in Asia, sloth bear of India and surrounding countries and the sun bear found in east Asia.

Taxonomically, bears are members of the order Carnivora (flesh-eating animals) which range in size from the tiny least weasel up to the giant polar bear. A distinctive characteristic of this group of animals is their four long canine teeth that are used for seizing prey and stabbing their victims.

WHO'S WHO: BROWNS, GRIZZLIES, POLARS

There was once a great deal of confusion in North America over what to call the brown bear or the grizzly bear and how many different species exist. This confusion existed not only among hunters but also among wildlife biologists and scientists. The scientific community has finally concluded that the brown bear and the grizzly bear are the same species, with the scientific name *Ursus arctos*.

The size difference among these bears is due to diet. Because of their high protein diet of salmon, the large coastal bear, commonly called brown bear, may grow to be 1,500 pounds or more; their inland brothers, commonly called grizzlies, generally weigh only up to 800 pounds.

There are only two subspecies of *Ursus arctos*. The brown-grizzly bears found on Kodiak, Afognak and Shuyak Islands are *Ursus arctos middendorffi*. All other brown-grizzly bears are *Ursus arctos horribilis*. Because of the difference in sizes of grizzly bears found along the Alaska coast, some hunter awards programs break the bears into two categories: brown bear and grizzly bear. We'll cover that in detail in Chapter 9 on trophies.

Because these names are the commonly accepted terminology used by most hunters and guides, I will use "brown bear" and "grizzly bear" in this book to discuss the large coastal bear and smaller inland bear, respectively. This also keeps with the Boone and Crockett Club scoring system. But please be aware: scientifically speaking, brown bears and grizzly bears are the same species.

The term "grizzly" probably comes from the mature bear's silver-tipped hair, or "grizzled" appearance. Early writers referred to the grizzly as the "white bear," and later many hunters, including Theodore Roosevelt, called it "Old Ephraim" or "ol' Eph," a commonly used name for the devil. However, some mountain men called it "grizzly," as is seen in Osborne Russell's book *Journal of a Trapper*. Mexicans called it "oso grande!"

Nomenclature of the polar bear is far less confusing. Its scientific name is *Ursus maritimus*. Eskimos gave the polar bear its first common name, Nanook, and Native Americans still use that term. It was English explorers who gave the white bear the name "polar bear."

Older grizzlies like this may have silver-tipped hair; thus the term "silvertip" grizzly.

BIG BEAR DISTRIBUTION

Grizzly range in the lower 48 states has been reduced to only six small areas.

GRIZZLIES & BROWNS

Grizzly bear distribution has changed greatly since the first Europeans came to North America. At that time, the range of the grizzly was extensive, covering Alaska, the Yukon, much of the Northwest Territories, British Columbia, Alberta, Saskatchewan and most of Manitoba.

In the Lower 48, the grizzly's range included all the western states east to the western edge of Minnesota and Iowa, most of Kansas and the western half of Oklahoma and Texas. Near Mexico, grizzly bears were found in the northern part of Baja California, and down through the central backbone of Mexico to Durango.

As civilization closed in on grizzly range, big bears were usually the first to go, partly because of their exaggerated reputation for being dangerous. It also didn't help that grizzlies took an occasional head of livestock for a meal. In many areas, the bears were forced to retreat simply because towns, ranches, railroads and highways invaded their solitude.

Lower 48 Grizzlies

Contrary to what many anti-hunters say, the demise of the grizzly in the Lower 48 was not the doing of sport hunters. The grizzly was shot, trapped and poisoned at every opportunity by those with business interests rather than by sport hunters. In fact, it has only been in fairly recent times that the grizzly has received recognition as a game animal to be managed.

Today, the range of grizzly bear is far less than what it was originally. There are few, if any, grizzlies left in Mexico. In the Lower 48, the grizzlies survive in six small areas:

1) In and adjacent to Yellowstone National Park.

2) Glacier National Park and the wilderness areas and associated lands south to the Blackfoot drainage and northwest to the Kootenai drainage in Montana.

3) The Cabinet Mountains and Yaak River drainage in the northwest corner of Montana.

4) The Bitterroot Mountains and associated wilderness lands north of the Salmon River and west to the Selway drainage in northern Idaho.

5) The Selkirk Mountains in northeast Washington and the panhandle of Idaho.

6) The northern edge of the Cascade Mountains in western Washington.

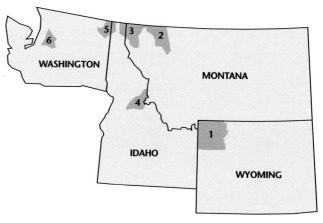

The six remaining Lower-48 areas that support grizzly bears.

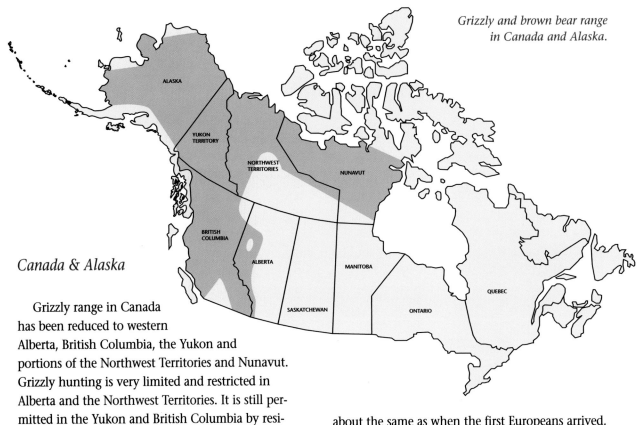

*Grizzly and brown bear range
in Canada and Alaska.*

Canada & Alaska

Grizzly range in Canada
has been reduced to western
Alberta, British Columbia, the Yukon and
portions of the Northwest Territories and Nunavut.
Grizzly hunting is very limited and restricted in
Alberta and the Northwest Territories. It is still permitted in the Yukon and British Columbia by residents and nonresidents.

The bright spot for both brown bears and grizzlies
in North America is Alaska, where the range is still
about the same as when the first Europeans arrived,
with the exception of areas inhabited by people. The
bear's population is still high, and hunting by
both residents and nonresidents is permitted.

Polar Bears

The distribution of the
polar bear has
changed very little
over time. Their range covers
the top of the world. In
North America, polar bears
are found along the Arctic
coastal regions from the
Seward Peninsula of Alaska
east to Labrador and south
along the shores of Hudson
Bay to James Bay.

*The polar bear's range has remained unchanged, stretching across the
Arctic coastline down to Hudson's Bay.*

IMPOSING PACKAGES INDEED

POLAR BEAR FACTS

For many years, the big brown bears found on Kodiak Island were thought to be the largest of bears, with recorded weights of up to 1,656 pounds and heights as tall as 11 feet.

But it is now thought that polar bears may be larger, as a rule, as one is on record at more than 11 feet tall and 2,210 pounds. Of course, this is an exceptional bear, and most polar bears taken by hunters fall in the 8- to 10-foot range. Mature males generally weigh between 600 and 1,200 pounds, and females 400 to 700 pounds. They stand about four feet high at the shoulder.

The polar bear's color is not pure white, as many people think, but is actually a yellowish-cream color. Each hair is hollow, insulating the bear from the extreme cold of its habitat. The polar bear's black nose stands out against the near-white background, and bears that are stalking seals have been observed placing a paw over the nose to camouflage it.

The polar bear's body shape is that of a sharp triangle with the apex at the nose, an ideal shape for cutting through water. The tapering head acts like the bow of a ship. When swimming, only the front feet, which are webbed, are used for paddling. The rear feet are used like rudders for steering. The polar bear can swim up to 60 miles, without resting, at an average speed of six miles per hour.

The polar bear must propel himself onto floating

Due to their high-protein fish diets, brown bears are generally larger for their age than inland grizzlies.

ice to capture unsuspecting seals. Polar bears can leap as high as 8 feet into the air from a swimming start. Stiff hair on the bottoms of polar bears' feet keep them from slipping on the ice. And polar bears' eyesight is much better than that of other bears.

GRIZZLY & BROWN BEAR FACTS

While the largest coastal Alaska brown bears are 10 feet or more in length and weigh more than 1,000 pounds, the average is in the 800- to 1,000-pound range. Those measuring more than 10 feet in length are getting harder to come by, and most hunters are glad to get a 9-foot bear. A large brown bear stands about 4 1/2 feet high at the shoulder.

Exceptional inland grizzlies may weigh up to 900 pounds, but the average is in the range of 400 to 800 pounds with an average length of 6 to 8 feet. They average 3 1/2 feet high at the shoulder. Females weigh one-half to three-quarters as much.

Brown and grizzly bears resemble their close relatives, black bears. But browns and grizzlies are usually larger, with prominent shoulder humps and longer, straighter claws than black bears. In profile, the faces of browns and grizzlies are concave between the forehead and the nose.

Color is not a very reliable way to differentiate between browns or grizzlies and black bears, because both species have many color phases. Brown and grizzly bears' colors range from dark brown to blond. Black bears' colors range from black to many hues of brown to blond.

TEETH & BONES

All the big bears have 42 teeth: 12 incisors, 4 canines, 16 premolars and 10 molars. Bears are the only large predators that regularly eat both plants and meat; therefore, they have both meat-eating and plant-eating teeth in their mouths. The molars are for grinding plant food, and the canine and incisor teeth are for catching and killing animals. The canine teeth of polar bears are longer than those of other big bears.

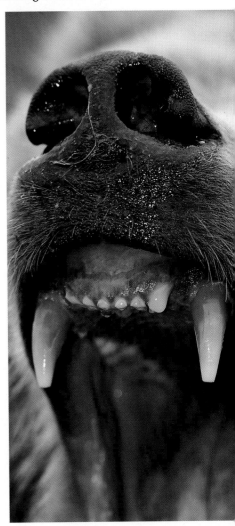

Bears are related to dogs, foxes and wolves, with a similar skeleton, except that the bones are larger and much heavier. Laced to this skeleton are massive muscles. Bears have a strong, unusually large heart, and big bears have been known to survive injuries that would kill any other animal.

The long claws on the front feet, some up to five inches, make any bear a formidable enemy and are very effective at digging up food or catching fish.

Bears have large canine teeth for catching and killing animals for food.

Above: Contrary to many hunters' beliefs, large bears can swim very well. Opposite page: Except for the mating period, big bears are loners. They don't want contact with other bears or man.

RUNNING, CLIMBING & SWIMMING

The body of the big bears may look fat and clumsy, but these animals are among the strongest and fastest on earth, running at speeds up to 40 miles per hour. Big bears can cover a distance of 150 yards in 10 seconds—a fact all hunters should keep in mind. Big bears also have tremendous endurance. I once interviewed an old grizzly hunter who had used dogs to hunt down grizzlies in the early 1900s. He said

Big Bear's Eyesight

Another misconception is that bears have very poor eyesight. I have heard people say with authority that bears are nearly blind. Biologists disagree. In fact, most think the bear's eyesight is as good as man's. Bears can see colors, form and movement, but apparently prefer to rely on their more acute senses of smell and hearing.

that on several occasions he had chased a grizzly for 30 miles before it came to bay.

A common myth about big bears is that they can't run downhill. Wrong! They can run downhill—or uphill—easily and quickly.

Due to the weight of mature brown and grizzly bears and the length of their claws, they have a hard time climbing trees, often preferring to shake their intended victim down or wait it out before attempting to climb. But as many hunters have learned the hard way, if the tree has limbs close enough for a bear to grab, he will come up.

There are also those who think heavy bears can't swim. Don't believe it; bears are excellent swimmers and can tolerate water much colder than a man can survive.

Big Bear's Longevity

The life span of big bears in the wild is from 20 to 25 years. What other big game animal lives so long? None. This is something to think about when you shoot a really big bear. Chances are that great animal has lived a long time and learned a lot along the way. Don't take him lightly, and hunt that dignified animal with respect.

PERSONALITY

The temperament of big bears is one of their least understood characteristics. Basically they are wilderness loners and don't want anything to do with man, or other bears (except for mating or rearing cubs).

Each bear, much more so than other members of the wild kingdom, seems to have its own personality. What one bear will do, another won't. What a bear will do today, he won't do tomorrow. This is why you can never predict a bear's behavior. They are known to possess a great amount of pride and dignity, and this alone has been suspected of causing some unsuspecting persons a lot of trouble. For example, a bear that is recovering from a fight with a larger bear may take his problems out on an unsuspecting person who happens along at the time.

Bears have been known to hold grudges against people. A bear that has been wounded by one hunter may take it out on several other hunters. Recorded incidents actually demonstrate this!

While polar bears may look at a man as just another large seal, browns and grizzlies are not generally man-eaters. When they attack (which is not nearly as often as most believe) there is usually a good reason—such as their being wounded, having cubs nearby, being startled, having food nearby, having their space invaded or just being mad at folks in general. If given a chance, most bears would rather just go their separate way.

BEAR CHOW TIME

The polar bear is the only North American bear that is nearly a true carnivore. His diet consists mainly of ringed seals, which he catches by slipping up on them or leaping out of the water on them at the edges of ice.

Polar bears also wait for seals at breathing holes. Young seals, a special treat for the bear, are caught by breaking into puppy chambers in snow on top of the ice in spring. Polar bears will also feed on bearded seals and carrion of whale, seal and walrus carcasses found along the coast. Polar bears occasionally eat small mammals, bird eggs and sometimes vegetation when other food is not available.

It might be easier to name what a brown or grizzly

Above: Grizzlies will eat almost anything, including carrion. Left: A polar bear hunting for its next meal.

bear won't eat than what he will. He is omnivorous. He likes all berries, green grass, horsetail, willow sedge, cow parsnip, pine nuts, fish, rodents, insects and roots of many plants. He also likes to eat domestic or game animals when he can get them, but he is probably not a significant predator of big game animals except during the spring moose and caribou calving season.

Browns and grizzlies especially like carrion and will feed on carcasses of animals. Occasionally a brown or grizzly will turn to cannibalism, especially liking small cubs. However, some wildlife biologists report that 90 percent of the bear's diet is vegetable matter. In settled areas, they will even eat garbage. I have learned the hard way that they like bacon, leftover bannock, beans, steak and most other camp foods, including canned goods.

Brown bears, grizzly bears and polar bears may consume as much as 90 pounds of food per day. If you're out hunting, make sure that 90 pounds doesn't come from your carcass!

THE LIFE CYCLES
OF BIG BEARS

There are two times when mature male bears break with their solitary lifestyles. One is when food is abundant near other bears (such as during the salmon run or when the berries are ripe); the other is when it's time to mate.

THE RUT: MATING SEASON

Polar bears, browns and grizzlies all breed in the spring. The polar bear's breeding season is March, April and May. Males actively seek out females by following their tracks on the sea ice. Brown and grizzly bear mating takes place from May through July, with the peak rutting activity in June. Big bears do not have strong ties, and a male will not stay with a female for long.

All female bears that breed have what biologists call "delayed implantation." That is, even though they breed in late spring or early summer, the fertilized egg does not implant in the uterus until October or November. Biologists believe this to be a survival

mechanism in that the embryo will not develop unless the sow is healthy and has sufficient fat reserved to last the winter and to care for the cubs. Delayed implantation and the short, six- to eight-week embryo development period means that the cubs are surprisingly small at birth, usually around one pound each.

DENNING & HIBERNATION

Once mating is completed, bears go their separate ways. As winter approaches, the bears begin to locate suitable denning sites. Polar bears seek out dens in late October and November, with most denning on land, but some on heavy sea ice. They seek the lee side of icebergs, steep hillside slopes where snowdrifts persist, or the lee side of lake or stream banks where deep snowdrifts accumulate.

Brown and grizzly bears usually

Where the soil is soft enough for digging, grizzlies will often excavate winter dens under large rocks like this.

locate their denning sites by late October, often selecting a site where the entrance is below a stand of willows or alders so that the hanging branches will cover the opening and catch the snow. Dens are sometimes found on north-facing slopes where snowdrifts are deeper.

Dens are usually located in soil that is soft enough for digging. The chamber is egg-shaped and large enough to allow the bear some room for stretching during the winter. It must be small enough, however, that the airspace will be efficiently warmed by the bear's body heat.

The winter dormancy period of bears differs from that of most other mammal hibernators because the body temperature does not drop. Brown and grizzly bears can remain inactive in dens for up to seven months by reducing their heart rate, metabolism functions, oxygen consumption and blood circulation. Among polar bears, pregnant females are the only ones that den for long periods of time.

CUBS

Young bears are born from late November through February. Except for polar bears, the cubs are born virtually naked. Cubs require a great deal of care from their mother. Polar bears will most often have a litter of two, and brown or grizzly bear litters may be from one to four, with an average of two.

Female polar bears and cubs break out of the den in late March or early April when the cubs weigh about 15 pounds. They make short trips to and from the den until the cubs become acclimated to the outside temperatures. Then they start traveling on the drifting sea ice. The cubs stay with their mother until they are about 28 months old. Females can breed again at about the time they separate from their cubs, so they generally produce litters every third year.

Brown and grizzly bears emerge from the den in about April, depending upon the weather. Females with cubs emerge later than single bears. The cubs

When polar bear cubs break out of their dens for a look at the outside world, they weigh about 15 pounds. This fellow has grown beyond that already, though, and probably weighs about 80 pounds.

Understanding Big Bears

Daily Movement

Daily movement of brown and grizzly bears is influenced by temperatures, as you would be if you had on a heavy, dark brown coat and were out in the sun for long periods. They move and feed during the cool evening and morning hours. They often prefer to feed in shady areas, making it harder for a hunter to spot them.

remain with their mother through their second year, and then the female will breed again.

Newborn cubs of brown, grizzly and polar bears are highly dependent on their mothers for protection from all dangers, including large male bears, which occasionally kill and eat cubs. The mother teaches her cubs hunting and feeding techniques. The cubs learn to recognize danger and to locate suitable denning sites. The mother is a very strict disciplinarian and quickly stops misbehavior with a hard blow from her paw.

During the second winter, the cubs den with their mother. They are chased off the following spring, as the mother is ready to breed again. Big bears usually become sexually mature between five and seven years of age.

A bear cub learns feeding techniques from its mother.

Habitat & Management

Habitat

Polar bear habitat is the Arctic ice pack and surrounding coastal areas. Brown and grizzly bear habitat is much more varied. When big bears descend from their dens in the spring in search of berries and grasses, they like riverbanks, flood plains and tidal flats. While a few bears use river shore trails and surrounding habitat during the early summer, they do not begin to concentrate there until berries (such as soapberries) ripen, and later when the salmon runs begin. Forest areas are used by big bears for shade and some food. But since many of the forests are so dense, the sunlight is restricted from reaching the forest floor, and adequate growth of vegetation suitable for food is limited.

In regions where a variety of forest and meadow types are found, there is a better supply of bear food than in the vast expanse of trees. Bears will feed in the meadows and make daybeds in the forest margins near open areas. Emerging greens adjacent to melting snow and moist creek edges are especially good for bear feeding. Roots, berries and ground squirrels make up the remainder of their diet. Where the forest thins at higher elevations and on snow slides, the slopes support shrubs, bushes and small, scattered tree growth. This is good grizzly habitat. The vast, open tundra is also home to brown and grizzly bears. This barren ground, which on first appearance seems void of any life, offers the big bears grasses, sedges, small mammals, and in some cases caribou calves, as food. Cover and shade are found in alder and willow thickets along creeks and lakes.

Big bears have a low reproduction rate. A mature grizzly sow will only produce offspring every two to three years.

MANAGEMENT

Big bear management knowledge is many years behind that of other big game species in North America. The public attitude toward the big bears has been one of fear and dislike. This has changed, though somewhat slowly in some areas, and now wildlife officials are working to learn more about bear management.

One factor that has to be taken into account, and one that many people don't consider, is the big bears' generally low rate of reproduction. We tend to think that all game animals are like deer. A healthy doe, often as young as a yearling, will produce two fawns each year; by contrast, there is usually a two- to three-year interval between litters in a female bear. On top of that, a female bear takes five

to seven years to reach sexual maturity in the first place. Also, bear reproduction can be greatly affected by food shortages; females in poor condition do not reproduce.

Because of this slow reproductive rate, game and fish agencies must conduct extensive studies on the total bear population to recommend desirable types of hunting at intensities that will not over-harvest populations. Research studies each year include detailed assessments of harvest, movement patterns, population surveys and basic life-history studies.

It is studies of this type that have produced the quota system for the hunting of big bears. This system, which dictates the number of bears that can be harvested in a specific area, has helped in keeping the bear population at healthy numbers, while allowing sportsmen to enjoy the resource.

It's All in the Habitat

Habitat conservation is another major part of any bear management program. Due to human development, the large tracts of wilderness required by big bears are ever-decreasing. Even where these vast areas exist, disturbances by man can have a major impact on bears. For example, an oil spill from a tanker in the Arctic may kill enough seals to lead to starvation of the polar bear in that area.

As more people invade bear habitat, the frequency of man-bear encounters is growing, and the bear is the ultimate loser. What most people in bear habitat don't realize is that they are in an area where man is not necessarily the supreme predator. Any management plan needs to guide human activities to avoid man-bear encounters. This may involve prohibiting man from using some areas at specific times.

As is pointed out in several places in this book, disturbance of bear habitat (by roads, oil rigs, mining, low-level aircraft activity and other development) forces bears into lower quality habitat where survival is difficult and reproduction is less successful. Land-controlling agencies must recognize these

challenges as a part of any big bear management program. Restrictions on agriculture, logging, mining and oil development may well be required in bear habitat. Without this, especially in Alaska, huntable bear populations will decline.

Big bear management is a relatively new science, and we still have much to learn about the management of these complex animals. We sportsmen can do our part by encouraging bear management programs and following hunting restrictions to the letter.

Bear encounters are becoming more frequent as more people venture into the backcountry.

Grizzly populations are diminishing along with the disappearance of the large blocks of undisturbed land that bears need.

Understanding Big Bears

Chapter Two

PLANNING THE HUNT

Y ou don't load up the old shotgun, whistle for the dog and head out the back door for a big bear hunt. This could be the outdoors event of a lifetime, and it takes a lot of work, planning and time to pull a hunt together. Plus, you will be spending major dollars to go on a big bear hunt. These instructions, tips and insights will help you make sure you plan correctly and completely ... so you get your money's worth and, bear or not, create great memories of a wonderful hunt in a grand land.

THE IMPORTANCE OF GOOD PLANNING

A hunt for big bears doesn't just happen. You need to plan well, and plan ahead, to make sure every aspect of your hunt is going to come off successfully. Poor planning can spell grief and even disaster when you're hunting big bears.

Look at it this way. You will spend a very big chunk of money to hunt big bears. It may be the hunt of a lifetime. It's certainly not a jaunt for whitetails in the back 40. Let's take a look at a true story, then talk about planning your hunt.

A True Story

Bob Perry had spent 10 years saving for a once-in-a-lifetime grizzly hunt. Both he and his wife had worked hard to put aside enough money for his dream hunt. At last the account was sufficient to hire a guide, pay the airfare and cover the license cost.

Bob picked out three guides to call by looking at ads in several of his favorite outdoor magazines. He picked the guides by the size of their ads, figuring that the more successful the guide, the more he could spend for advertising.

The first guide he called was polite but almost 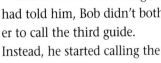 sounded as if he were talking him out of the hunt. He told Bob that his hunter success ran 60 percent on his most recent spring hunt. He pointed out that his hunts were hard, with days often spent in snowshoes.

He told Bob that his camps were comfortable but not like a Hilton, and that there was an additional cost to fly from the nearest village served by commercial airlines to his base camp. Bob figured this must be a trapper picking up some side money by guiding in the spring.

The second guide he called sounded more like what he wanted. He told Bob that he achieved a 99 percent success rate every season on bears, and due to the abundance of bears in the area, Bob might have time to get in some fishing. The guide described the terrain as gentle and the camp as new and modern in every way. As the guide gave Bob three references, he assured him of success if he hunted with him.

Excited over what this guide had told him, Bob didn't bother to call the third guide. Instead, he started calling the second guide's three references.

The first reference was someone in Las Vegas. His report on the guide was that everything was excellent, first class, bears everywhere. His closing comment was that his brother-in-law ran the best hunting business in Alaska. The second reference was never home. The third reference was actually a fisherman who said that he had seen lots of bear sign when he fished with this guide.

In the meantime, the guide sent Bob a brochure, which showed pictures of bears and had many statements from hunters about how good the guide service was. Bob, running short of time, decided that the guide must be all right and sent him a 50 percent deposit.

That was the last Bob heard of his guide until about a month before the scheduled hunt, when Bob called him to get information on clothing and hunting licenses. The guide told him to pack as if he were going on a whitetail deer hunt and he would be okay. He further told him that licenses were no problem and they would take care of those details when he got to Alaska.

Things Get Bad

Soon the time for the hunt arrived. Bob flew from his home in Kentucky to Anchorage, and from there to the small village near the guide's camp. The airport at the village was a small metal building, and when Bob arrived, there was no one to meet him. In fact, a few minutes after the commercial airliner departed, there was no one else at the building at all.

The locals who got off the plane had all gone home, and Bob was left standing in the cold building, watching the snow fall outside and wondering what he should do.

Walking around, he came upon an aircraft mechanic working in a hangar adjacent to the small terminal. The mechanic knew where the guide's base camp was. He told Bob he was the local air taxi, but he couldn't take him out to the camp until the next morning. He suggested that Bob get a cab and go into the village to stay at Porter's Motel.

Bob, somewhat bewildered at this point, had the mechanic call a cab, which turned out to be a beat-up pickup that cost $50 for the three-mile trip to the mobile home called Porter's Motel. The cold,

Planning the Hunt

somewhat-less-than-clean room cost $95 per night. The only café open charged eight bucks for a small hamburger.

Bob had not expected any of these costs, and they were eating into his extra cash. The next morning, after waiting around for two hours, he was wedged with his gear into the rear seat of a Super Cub and flown into the base camp—at a cost of $200. At that point, though, he was just glad to get there.

As Bob got his gear from the plane, the guide walked up and introduced himself. In almost the same breath, he asked for the cashier's check for the balance of the hunt cost. As they walked over to the tent camp, Bob was shocked at what he saw: a tent shantytown. Stopping at one tent, the guide told Bob this would be his "cabin." Inside were two army cots with badly-stained mattresses. The tent was heated with an oil-burning stove that left an odor of diesel

fuel in the tent.

The cook tent was the guide's headquarters, and there Bob learned that he was the only hunter on this hunt. As he ate a bowl of greasy stew, the guide asked about his hunting license. Surprised, Bob told him he had waited until arrival to get it as the guide had suggested. "Oh, I meant to get it in the village when you arrived there," the guide told him. "I'll fly you back there this afternoon in my plane to get it, but I'll have to charge you $250 for this service."

It Gets Worse

The next seven days were the worst in Bob's life. He was constantly wet and cold from the lack of the right equipment. The guide never left camp; instead, a young man (who admitted he had never guided in this area before) walked with Bob from daylight until dark. Their lunches were light, and they only had creek water to drink with lunch. Breakfast and dinner were always greasy and never enough. Bob got very little sleep, as the fumes in his tent were so bad he had to keep the flaps open, resulting in temperatures colder than his sleeping bag was designed to handle. He saw little bear sign and never saw a bear.

On the way home, there were several delays in flights, which required him to stay overnight both at the village and in Anchorage, and cost him a lot more than he had ever expected. Bob returned home dejected, broke and almost a physical wreck. It would take him a long time to get over his hunt.

This is a true story. The names were changed for obvious reasons. But the message is also obvious: The secret to any hunt, especially a hunt for big bears, is to put in a lot of time and careful thought planning the hunt. There is much to consider as you put the hunt together, and *the success or failure of the hunt can be determined by your planning.*

Properly planning a bear hunt is the first step in having a lot of time to hunt and seeing a sight like this. Good planning and hunting success go together.

PLAN EARLY, PLAN HARD

ear hunts cannot be thrown together within a month or two. First of all, bear guides with good reputations for running top-notch hunts are often booked a year or more in advance. Some of the best ones will be booked two or more years in advance. Second, there are so many things to consider when planning the bear hunt that a great deal of time is needed. It is best to start at least two years in advance of when you want to hunt.

WHICH BEAR?

The logical starting point when planning a big bear hunt is determining which of the big bears you want to hunt: polar, grizzly or brown.

Polar Bear

The polar bear is a much-desired trophy for all of us who enjoy bear hunting. But hunting opportunities are limited. Of course, cost is one limiting factor. As of this writing, a polar bear hunt will run you from $18,000 to $22,000. That's a chunk of change!

There's another limiting factor too: where you can hunt. The Marine Mammal Protection Act of 1972 prohibits U.S. citizens from hunting polar bears in Alaska. Natives can hunt and are allowed a quota of bears, but these tags cannot be sold. So—you won't be hunting polar bear in Alaska.

Canada's Northwest Territories presents the only North American opportunity where a U.S. citizen can hunt polar bears and bring home his or her trophy. The two huge units open to this hunting are north of the 60th parallel. The polar bear population in these areas is healthy and can withstand the limited harvest allowed.

Jerome Knap of Canada North Outfitting conducts 45 to 50 polar bear hunts a year around the coast of the Baffin Island, Southampton Island, southern Ellesmere Island, northern Victoria Island and Lancaster Sound. Knap, having hunted over much of the world himself, considers the polar bear hunt the greatest hunting adventure available today. It means going out on the polar ice, living there in igloos or tents with Eskimo guides, and meeting the bear on its own terms. By international law, polar bear hunts today have to be conducted by traditional means, with dog sleds being the only mode of transportation the hunter can use.

Knap cautions that the polar bear hunter has to face brutal elements.

A polar bear rarely sits still, and can easily cover 60 miles in a day.

Temperatures are usually well below zero both day and night. Blizzards, fog and "white-outs" of frozen ice crystals can occur. At times, polar bears are found only near the floe edge—where sea ice and open water meet. Hunting here has to be done very cautiously because ice frequently moves. The guides must be thoroughly experienced in traveling in these types of elements, says Knap.

"Going on a polar bear hunt is like going on a minor Arctic expedition before the age of aircraft," says Knap. The hunter and his guide must be equipped for virtually every emergency the terrain and elements may throw at them. Canada North Outfitting's guides pack food for at least 20 days in case they become stuck in a blizzard. Two-way radios with insulated battery packs are also carried in case of emergency.

A polar bear is nearly always on the move—hunting. An adult bear can trot all day, easily covering 60 miles. Knap says the highly mobile nature of the animal makes it even more difficult to hunt. However, the success rate on Knap's polar bear hunts is high—about 90 percent. "But that's because the Canada North Outfitting guides are willing to work hard, sometimes from dawn to dusk," says Knap.

There are two periods when it is possible to hunt polar bears: in early winter from late October to early November, and the main hunting season from mid-March to late May. Before late October, the sea ice is not firm enough to support dog teams and sleds. By late November, the fury of winter has set in and there is almost total darkness.

Bear hunting begins again in March as daylight hours lengthen and the temperatures become more moderate. Then bears start to move about and hunt seals. After late May, the snow may become too soft for the sled. Also, by late May, the bears start to lose their long winter coats and the skins are no longer in their best condition. The legal polar bear season traditionally ends May 31.

If you're willing to invest the dollars to hunt polar bears, the Northwest Territories is the only place to do it. The only other frontier to try would be Siberia. But the international travel presents an extra challenge, and you won't be able to bring a trophy back, so there's little reason to go.

Alaska Brown Bears

The brown bear—also known as the coastal grizzly or Kodiak bear, whichever you prefer—is popular for those who want a very large bear for their trophy room. Hunting this bear is done along the coast of southern Alaska in a land that is waterlogged and thickly covered with vegetation.

These hunts can be physically and mentally demanding, especially if hunting on foot. On brown bear hunts I have spent hours walking through thick alders where vision was limited to 10 feet or less. On the same hunts, I have spent other days wading rushing streams to get up mountainsides where the big bears were feeding.

Other hunts, with guides who use boats as their principal means of transportation, can be much less demanding.

For hunters who are not in good shape, a boat hunt can be less physically demanding.

Guides for coastal bears are usually booked at least a year in advance, and at this writing, hunts cost $8,000 to $15,000. Based on a survey I conducted among outfitters, success rates average around 80 percent.

Grizzly Bears

The interior grizzly is a trophy of a lifetime, and quite often these bears are much more aggressive than their larger cousins, the brown bears. Hunting for the grizzly may be conducted in many ways. Days are often spent sitting on a high point glassing valleys and mountains slopes. During

Planning the Hunt

When hunting grizzlies, be prepared to spend lots of time walking and looking, walking and looking. Your feet and your binoculars will be your allies.

some spring hunts, you may spend long days traveling on snowshoes or floating icy rivers in an inflatable boat. Most fall grizzly hunts are part of a combination hunt for moose, caribou and/or Dall sheep.

Grizzly hunts are generally a little less expensive than brown bear hunts if grizzly is the only species hunted. At this writing, hunts range from about $8,000 to $12,000. Hunter success on grizzlies varies from guide to guide, with a spring season success average of around 75 percent and a fall season average of about 50 percent. I think in any season a 50 percent success rate is what hunters should expect.

SPRING OR FALL?

Once you've decided which bear you want to hunt, the next question to answer is whether you want to hunt in the spring or fall. In the case of the polar bear, you have no choice; you go when you can get a hunt. Grizzly and brown bear hunters often prefer the spring season so they can find an animal whose pelt is not rubbed.

While spring bears seem

to have the better pelts, I have seen bears fresh out of the wintering den that had bad rubs. In areas where snow is on the ground in the spring and hunters can travel on snowshoes, the spring season can be best for the hunter who is in good shape and is willing to work hard for his bear. On spring grizzly hunts I know of out of Koyuk on Alaska's Seward Peninsula, most hunters who are in good shape and are willing to hunt hard on snowshoes fill their tags.

On the other hand, weather can play a major role in determining when is the best time to hunt during the spring. It is very easy to be a week too early and not see a bear. If you're a week too late, the insects will eat you up and the bear you see may be rubbed.

Where bears are feeding on salmon, the fall hunt is the preference of many hunters simply because the bears are concentrated along streams. Some guides who hunt moose like to have grizzly hunters during the fall, as they can hunt "moose kills" which attract bears. When you are hunting grizzlies as part of a combination hunt, the guide will often hunt the other species first, taking a grizzly if and when spotted while looking for other game.

There are good and bad points associated with both spring and fall bear hunts, and the individual must decide which points are the most important to him. I personally don't have a preference. I have hunted both seasons successfully, and bad weather has ruined hunts for me during both seasons. As

Study a bear carefully before making the decision to shoot. Is the pelt rubbed? Spring is the best season for locating unrubbed bears like this one.

Many bear hunters save time scouting and opt for the fall grizzly season when bears spend a lot of time along salmon streams.

North country was that large expanses of land are void of game animals during periods of the year. Vast herds of caribou aren't found in every valley, nor is there a bear in every alder thicket. In conjunction with perhaps no other species of game is the word "hunting" more aptly used than in bear hunting.

Many other factors make picking out hot spots for bear hunting difficult. Some areas are closed to bear hunting on relatively short notice, and others are restricted to residents only or are only open in some years. In some areas, such human activity as timber cutting and mining cause the bear population to move on. It is for all these reasons that bear hunters should get a good guide and depend on him to sort out the movement of bears, whims of bureaucrats and impact of "progress" on the land.

with all hunting, we also need some luck to go along with our skillfully made decisions. Whether you can be gone from home for two weeks may have a lot to do with your decision, as well as the advice of the guide you choose to work with.

BEST AREAS

One of the questions most often asked by prospective bear hunters is, "Where are the best areas to hunt bears?" I think what they mean to ask is, "Where are bears most numerous?" To answer that question, we must understand a couple of facts.

Bears Are Scattered

First, big bears are wanderers. They like to be alone, and an area that may have several bears in it today may not contain a single bear tomorrow.

Second, the first-time hunter to the Far North must know that this vast country is not wall-to-wall with bears or any other critters. I think the greatest shock I had when I first started working in the Far

Be prepared to spend long hours without seeing a bear. Bears are wanderers, and it may take a few days to find a trophy. Be ready at all times.

STATES & PROVINCES

In order to evaluate the overall big bear situation in North America, let's take a look at each political subdivision and the current bear situation there:

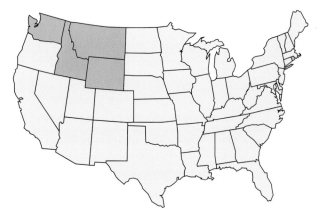

Lower 48

Montana was the last state in the Lower 48 to offer grizzly bear hunting, but that opportunity ended when the bears were put on the endangered species list. Bears are coming back into Montana as well as Wyoming—but with them so are some of the problems associated with having a top-rung predator around. Yet until Lower-48 grizzlies are delisted and management is handed back to the individual states, there won't be any legal hunting seasons. You'll have to go to the Far North to get your griz.

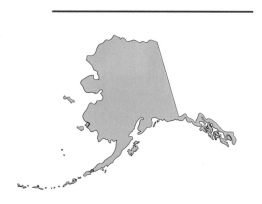

Alaska

The Alaska Department of Fish and Game does not differentiate between interior grizzlies and coastal brown bears; they are all brown bears. The population of brown bear there hovers in the 32,000 to 43,000 range. The total kill is usually around

1,200 or so browns, with the three top game management units being unit 9, the Alaska Peninsula area; unit 8, the Kodiak Archipelago; and unit 13, the area north of Valdez. There is no doubt that Alaska gives the best opportunity for bear hunting in North America.

British Columbia

This is the second-best bet for a grizzly, as the estimated grizzly population in British Columbia is 5,000 to 8,000 bears. Most of the coast and northern mountains of British Columbia offer good hunting. The harvest is on a tightly controlled quota system, which has done a lot to improve the grizzly situation.

Yukon Territory

The Yukon has an estimated grizzly population of between 6,000 and 7,000 bears, which is widely scattered throughout the territory. On average, 85 grizzlies are taken each year by hunters. Guided, nonresident hunters account for most of this harvest, taking about 50 bears each year. Much of the Yukon

Territory is not an especially good area for a bear-only hunt. It is, however, a good idea to have a grizzly tag if you are hunting other big game species, as this is when you are most likely to encounter one.

Northwest Territories & Nunavut

Grizzlies are found in about 75 percent of the Northwest Territories and Nunavut, excluding the dense forests of the south. Provincial grizzly biologists have no estimate of the number of grizzlies here because of the vastness of the provinces and the fact that much of the area is uninhabited. For some time this huge area, which comprises roughly one-third of Canada, was closed to nonresident bear hunters. That is changing, as natives of several communities are beginning to guide sport hunters rather than take their quota of bears for subsistence use. The number of bear tags issued to nonresident sport hunters is limited to a small quota, however. This is the only area in North America open to polar bear hunting, so it is the best.

Alberta

Grizzly bears number only about 800 in Alberta, so the harvest is very limited and open only to residents.

Specific Areas to Hunt

As a general rule, there are some areas that are considered especially good, and with a twinge of reluctance, I will mention them. However, keep in mind, as I have pointed out several times in this book, browns, grizzlies and polar bears are lone wanderers and there are no permanent hot spots.

For big-bodied browns, the central and southern sections of the Alaska Peninsula are good. For record-book browns, the Kodiak Archipelago (which includes Kodiak, Raspberry and Afognak Islands) is your best bet. On Kodiak Island alone there are between 2,000 and 3,000 brown bears. Many Boone and Crockett record book bears have been taken in this area.

The best bets for grizzlies are in British Columbia and Alaska. In British Columbia, the coastal areas around Bella Coola and Kemano are tops, as are the Cassiar Mountains in the north central part of the province. In Alaska, the Cooper River area, Seward Peninsula, the headwaters of the Kuskokwim River and some parts of the Brooks Range are considered very good.

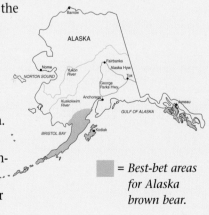

= Best-bet areas for Alaska brown bear.

Planning the Hunt

SELECTING A GUIDE

Once you have decided which bear you want to hunt, the time of the year, the state or province, whether to use rifle, pistol or bow, the amount of money you can spend, and if you want to hunt other big game or not, it is time to start looking for a guide. This may be a time-consuming part of the planning process, but it is critical to your success that it be done with care.

GUIDE NEEDED

To hunt big bears, you are required by law to have a guide unless you are a resident of the state or province. (This is unlike the requirements for hunting most other big game animals, except sheep.) Since most of us aren't residents of the areas we will hunt, I won't discuss do-it-yourself hunts or drop-camp hunting. Most of us will have to employ a guide, and it behooves us to get the best one we can for our hunt.

Members of the North American Hunting Club are fortunate to have a member magazine, *North American Hunter*, which publishes hunting reports on guides that Club members have used on hunts. These reports give the names and addresses of the guides, and the members rate the guides on such factors as hunting services and accommodations.

The North American Hunting Club also has available to its members a booklet called "NAHC Approved Outfitters and Guides." It lists guides and outfitters from the United States and Canada who have been approved by the majority of the Club members hunting with them. These two Club services are good places to start getting names of guides to contact.

The next best source is friends who have hunted with guides. Many of the best bear guides run small operations, and thanks to their success and efforts at running a good service, need little or no advertising. Word of mouth from satisfied clients keeps them booked well in advance. These guides can be selec-

tive in the clientele they accept, and they may check you out as well as *you* check *them* out.

Hunting shows attract guides who have booths or displays promoting their hunts. By attending one of these events, you can meet a number of guides face-to-face.

One of the less desirable places to select a guide is out of the "guides and outfitters" section of outdoor magazines. You must keep in mind that anyone with enough money can run an enticing ad. Some of the worst guides I've hunted with ran the most alluring ads.

Many big bear guides and outfitters have booths at hunting shows. This gives you a chance to discuss your hunt expectations in detail.

which bear you want to hunt and which hunting season you have in mind. If you want to hunt other big game species, you should tell him so at this time. You should make it clear to him up front if you plan to hunt with a handgun, muzzleloader or bow; it may save both of you some time if he only takes modern rifle hunters.

If you have any physical limitations that would require you to hunt using a specific technique, such as by boat or from a blind, you should let him know that early in the conversation. The more he knows about you, the better he can inform you about the services he can or cannot offer.

Open Up Communication

Once you select a list of bear hunting guides you are interested in, write to each of them for their literature. This will give you a little more information to study about each outfit and help you ask specific questions when you go to the next step of the selection process, which is a phone conversation with each guide.

Keep in mind when calling guides that most of them spend a good portion of their time in various hunting or fishing camps or running traplines. They are seldom readily available to come to the phone when you call, so you may have to try again and again. If you leave a message, don't be discouraged if you don't get a return call for a few days or even a few weeks. It may be weeks before the guide is back to his home or office to get phone messages.

Phone Interview

The best way to go about a phone interview with guides is to write up a questionnaire. This way you will not omit some important questions, and after all the interviews are complete, you can compare the answers.

Begin your interview by introducing yourself and telling the guide where you are from. Tell the guide

Good Questions to Ask

Once he knows something about you and what you expect, it's time for you to start asking questions—lots of questions. Here are some of the questions you should ask:

1. Where exactly does he bear hunt?
2. What is the terrain like in that area(s)?
3. What is the weather usually like during the time you want to hunt?
4. What hunting techniques are used for bears?
5. Will he or someone else guide you? What is their experience?
6. How long has he been guiding bear hunters? In the area(s) mentioned?
7. How many hunters does he take at one time?
8. What is the camp like? Base camp? Spike camp?
9. What is the guide-to-hunter ratio?
10. How many actual hunting days are included?
11. How do you get to spike camps? (You can't fly and hunt the same day.)
12. What is the cost of this hunt? *Exactly* what does that cover? What *doesn't* it cover?

Planning the Hunt

Before calling a guide or his references, have your questions written out and be ready to take notes on the answers. Getting a satisfactory hunt requires research.

13. What about transportation between the airport and the base camp? Who arranges it, and is there an additional charge?
14. Is there an additional cost for preparing a trophy for the trip home?
15. Are there any additional expenses? Ask this question at least twice.
16. When does he consider the best time to hunt bears there? Are there openings then?
17. What are the sizes of the bears taken there? Ask both pelt and skull size.
18. What equipment is the hunter expected to furnish?
19. Ask for the names and addresses of two hunters who hunted with him last year and were successful, then two who were not successful.
20. What was his hunter success rate on bears last year? The last five years?

Thank the guide for his time and tell him you will get back to him after you check out his references.

Call References

Next, call the references, including any NAHC members who may have hunted with him. Again, be well organized with written questions. And again—keep trying. Most of these people will be more than willing to help you out, but their schedules may be very busy.

After introducing yourself and asking permission to discuss their hunt with XYZ guide service, begin asking these questions.

1. How would they rate their overall hunt?
2. Were they successful? If so, what was the size of the bear and distance of the shot?
3. How many hunters were in the base camp? Spike camp?
4. How was the food? Lodging? Guide's equipment?
5. Was there enough help in camp?
6. Was the hunt well organized?
7. Who was their guide? How would they rate him?
8. What hunting technique was used?
9. What form of transportation was used to get to spike camps? To and from the airport?
10. Were there any hidden costs?
11. What was the weather like? The terrain?
12. How many bears did they see?
13. What did they not like about the hunt?
14. Did the guide do a good job with the pelt and skull?
15. Would they hunt with him again?

A Word on Success Rates

Save guide question number 20 for last so you can discuss the hunter success rate at length if necessary and compare it to the discussion that has already taken place. Hunter success rate will often tell you a lot about a guide. If he tries to fudge on this vital statistic, watch him. I have had guides tell me they had an 80 percent success rate. When the truth came out, that figure was for *all* species of big game; the success rate for *bears* was only 20 percent. Some guides—these don't usually stay in business long—will tell you whatever they think you want to hear. I like specifics, such as how many bear hunters he had last year and how many of them actually got a bear. Most guides will be honest with you on this, but there are always a few bad apples in the barrel.

Remember the first guide Bob Perry called at the beginning of this chapter, the one who Bob thought was trying to talk him out of booking a hunt? He was probably Bob's best bet. When a guide will point out to you the negative points of the hunt as that one did, he's probably being honest, and his candor was definitely a mark in his favor. Bob certainly made a mistake in not researching this guide further.

16. What equipment did they not have that they wish they had taken?

By the time you have answers to these questions from four different people, you will most likely have a good idea about the guide and his operation. Remember to talk to both successful hunters as well as ones who didn't shoot a bear.

FINAL DECISION

Now you must decide whether you want to bet several thousand dollars on a guide. Assuming you decide to go with one, you should call right away to let him know your decision and discuss dates and costs in detail. Be sure to find out what his deposit and cancellation policies are. This is especially true when planning a year or more in advance.

Request a contract spelling out the details of your transaction, including cancellation policy, deposit and final payment information. While you are on the phone with him, ask what calibers and loads he prefers so you can start preparing; it's never too early! Also, request a detailed what-to-bring list so that you can begin to gather the needed gear.

When you hang up, you should immediately send him a letter spelling out your understanding of your arrival and departure dates from his camp, total cost, deposit and final payment, including when and how final payment will be made (usually upon arrival by cashier's check) and cancellation agreement. This will let him see in writing what you understand the deal to be, and if there is any misunderstanding, you can get it straightened out quickly.

If you book a hunt a year or more in

advance, you should talk to the guide every few months, just to stay in touch. Guides, like all business owners, go bankrupt, lose their territory, die, get ill, and so on, and you should look after your deposit. In addition, you'll get to know him better, keep up with his hunting success, and set up a rapport.

You may find it difficult to book the guide you really wanted, as he has filled up his hunts. If so, try to get on his waiting list. When I was in the business, I had cancellations every year and maintained a waiting list to fill those openings. Many happy, successful hunters have gone home with bears because they were willing to wait on a list.

Since a guide is required for you to hunt big bears, get the best guide you can by taking the time to call references. Success comes with having a highly qualified guide who will work for you to get you a trophy.

KNOW ALL COSTS

An important step in the planning process is to determine as much of the cost of your bear hunt as you can. Many hunters inexperienced at hunting the Far North mentally accept the cost of booking the hunt to be about all of the expenses. This can be a trap.

OTHER TRAVEL EXPENSES

In addition to the cost of the hunt, expect necessary hunting licenses to be another $400 to $500 or more. Round-trip commercial airfare, depending on where you're flying from, might be another $800-plus. There could be an air taxi or charter flight cost, ranging between $200 and $500 each way, for trans-

portation to the guide's camp.

More often than not, the remoteness of Far North hunting camps means traveling at least one day before and after your hunt. Accommodations and meals for those days might run another $300 or more. It is not at all uncommon to be weathered-in along the route, which can cost as much as $200 per day for room and meals.

I have spent as many as five days in a small village waiting for the weather to break, paying top dollar for a tiny room and overcooked hamburgers. These delays weren't in the hunting plans at all.

If you are successful on the hunt, there might be an extra charge for the additional baggage (skin and skull) on your return trip. This could amount to $75,

$100 or more. If you took advantage of a special booking price on your commercial airline tickets that imposes a penalty for making schedule changes, a delay in getting out of camp because of weather can mean some stiff additional charges.

Several years ago, I had been hunting in a bear camp in British Columbia for two weeks. Our hunt was successful, and we came out of the bush right on time to stay with our flight schedule. At the little airport where we were to catch our commercial flight, we learned that United Airlines, on which our return flights were booked, was crippled by a pilots' strike. To make a long story short, it took us three days to get home ... at an enormous cost we hadn't expected.

Looking at what can and often does happen, you can see that the $8,000 grizzly hunt in reality costs $10,000 to $12,000. Not all hunts, thank goodness, run into all these problems and extra costs, but it happens often enough that you should look for the hidden costs in your planning and carry some extra travelers' checks with you. Don't depend on credit cards; I've been in some remote settlements where charter services, hotels and restaurants didn't accept credit cards.

Be sure you have a clear understanding of where to get these licenses, then do it before the hunt if possible. Standing in the middle of an airstrip at base camp is the wrong time to find out that the nearest hunting license vendor is 150 miles away. Don't assume anything. Your guide should be able to provide all this information.

Other Services

As mentioned earlier, press your guide to tell you exactly what services his fee does and does not include and the costs of additional services. Some guides charge extra for preparing trophies to be flown out. There may also be other additional charges, such as for additional days in camp due to getting weathered in. Your contract should spell all this out.

Tips

Another expense that is entirely optional but frequently included is a tip for your guide and/or other camp personnel. Since it is not obligatory, the

OTHER COST CONSIDERATIONS

While a lot of these costs can't be planned for, such as getting weathered-in along the way, some thoughtful planning can cut your surprises down to a minimum.

Licenses

Get all the hunting license information from your guide in advance. Find out if you need a general and/or big game nonresident license in addition to a polar, brown or grizzly license. Ask what, if any, special permits are required. Find out the total cost of all the necessary licenses, permits, etc. When should you get them and where?

Know what services and equipment your guide will provide. You don't want to start your hunt in some remote camp without a sleeping bag when you were expected to furnish your own.

51

amount of any tip you want to give is also up to you. However, a common amount given to a guide who has done a good job and helped you get a trophy is at least $100. Even if your hunt has not been successful but you feel that the guide has given exceptional effort, a tip is proper.

Other camp personnel who are frequently tipped include wranglers who have been helpful to you, base camp cooks who prepare good meals, camp-hands who might flesh and care for your bear skins, and anyone else whose special effort you would like to reward. A common amount for these people is at least $50.

It has been my experience as both a guide/outfit-ter and big game hunter that the owner of the guiding service is not usually tipped, even if he is the one who guides you. Hunters do frequently give gifts, such as outdoor equipment, to the owner/guide, either while they are there or by mail after the hunt. It is not at all uncommon for hunters to leave a piece of equipment that they used on the hunt, such as a hunting knife, binoculars or extra ammunition, with the owner/guide, especially in the Far North where equipment is harder to come by.

Shipping Trophies

Be sure to check with your travel agent concern-

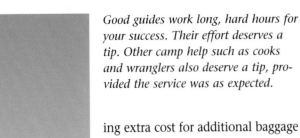

Good guides work long, hard hours for your success. Their effort deserves a tip. Other camp help such as cooks and wranglers also deserve a tip, provided the service was as expected.

ing extra cost for additional baggage in the event you are returning with a big bear pelt and skull. Also know and understand your options if you don't make your return schedule on time.

PLANNING FOR THE UNEXPECTED

After getting into several uncomfortable situations because of unplanned, unexpected costs on Far North hunting trips, I now make it a policy to carry an additional $1,500 in travelers' checks and $500 U.S. or Canadian cash, depending on where

I'm going, to meet these unforeseen eventualities. This is in addition to what I *think* I will need. It has come in handy several times.

Another precaution I now take is to get the name, address and phone number of someone the guide knows in the town or village I fly into nearest his camp. In the event I am suddenly stuck in a remote village that is not really equipped for tourists, I have someone who will give me a hand getting my problems solved. Also, if the guide's contact likes you, you can sometimes save a lot of money on room cost, meals, ground transportation and other expenses.

Some hunters I know send their firearms and hunting gear by airfreight, insured, to their guide a week or two early to make sure it's there when they arrive. Like many other hunters, I have had to borrow clothes and a gun on a hunt because my luggage didn't arrive when I did. The mishandling of luggage happens, and it is good to work out a plan with your guide to have your gear sent to the camp early.

Consider shipping your rifle to your outfitter a week or two before your hunt to make your travel much easier.

Planning the Hunt

Chapter Three

CONDITIONING FOR THE HUNT

*I*f you fail to condition yourself physically for a big bear hunt, you will go home empty-handed. This chapter shows you how to prepare your body for this very exhilarating but exhausting task. But don't forget about preparing your mind for the rigors of a big bear hunt. How you think and act and react will also affect your hunt's outcome. The country is big and often bleak; you'll go many days without seeing game. Here's how to prepare yourself mentally for what's ahead.

PHYSICAL CONDITIONING

The importance of conditioning your body for the hunt cannot be overemphasized.

Regardless of how well the bear hunter can shoot, how good his guide may be or how many bears are in the area, if the hunter is not in good—I mean *very good*—physical and mental condition, his chances for success are slim.

When I surveyed guides throughout big bear country, the most common reason they gave for bear hunters not being successful was that the hunters were not in good physical or mental condition for the hunt. We'll cover physical conditioning in this section, and mental strength later.

A PHYSICAL CHALLENGE

Contrary to some opinions, big bear hunting is not easy. In fact, a polar bear hunt by dogsled is gen-erally considered the most demanding hunt in North America. Grizzly and brown bear hunting run a close second, being on par with sheep hunting.

When you embark on long days of walking on soggy ground wearing hip boots, days in deep snow wearing snowshoes, climbing steep mountains and crossing roaring streams, often carrying your camp on your back, you had better be in good condition. Your guide, who will be in shape, will want to work hard to get you a bear, but he can't do his job effectively if you can't keep up.

I have been on many hunts where a hunter who thought he was in good shape would give up the hunt after two or three days. I once saw an entire group of five hunters call off their hunt after only two days of hunting. They hadn't gotten off to a good start when blisters, obesity and lack of endurance did them in. Two other hunters, both in good shape and working out of the same base camp, took near-record-book bears by the sixth day and saw a total of seven bears.

IT'S ALL IN THE LEGS

Because bears are wanderers, it takes a lot of searching to find one, and in most cases, that means a lot of walking. That requires strong legs, not only for going up hills, but perhaps more important, for coming down steep hills. Because you will likely be carrying a backpack or a daypack, wearing lots of clothes, pulling yourself up steep slopes, fighting alders, etc., your upper body should also be strong and in peak shape.

You should choose a guide who uses a hunting technique that is compatible with your physical condition. If you feel that long hard walks over steep terrain are out, you may want to opt for a guide who uses horses or boats for transportation. However, if you don't normally ride horses, that activity can be rough on the body. Using a boat for spotting is often the least physically demanding of the hunting techniques.

GETTING IN SHAPE

The best way to prepare physically is to begin getting your body in shape months before the hunt date. There are literally hundreds of workout

Bear hunting can require lots of walking, sometimes up mountains, sometimes in boggy, wet tidal flats. Strengthen your legs in preparation for your hunt.

programs in print that are supposed to put your body back in shape, but the best program I've ever tried was developed by North American Hunting Club Member Dennis Campbell. Campbell is a pharmacist who devotes a lot of time each year to hunting big game throughout North America, and is an official measurer for the Boone and Crockett Club and for Safari Club International.

Early in his big game hunting career, Campbell noticed that the various conditioning programs he tried didn't really prepare him for the rigors of his hunts. He also noticed that his positive mental attitude toward the hunt was directly related to the condition of his body for each hunt. Because of his dissatisfaction with existing conditioning programs, Campbell set out to develop his own, utilizing his

formal education in pharmacy and his background as a college athlete.

His goal was a fitness program that was simple and flexible, yet prepared him for bear, sheep, goat or any other type of hunting which might involve lots of difficult walking, climbing, backpacking and horseback riding. After several years of trial and error, he finally came up with a conditioning program that is simple, yet provides him outstanding results. I have also followed this routine and can attest to its effectiveness. While Campbell's program might not be right for you, you might find it useful in planning your own.

The Program

Campbell's conditioning program consists of four basic exercises and two occasional or substitute exercises. The four basic ones are jumping rope, pushups, bicycling and walking. The occasional exercises are climbing stairs and jogging.

Campbell considers *jumping rope* the most beneficial activity in a hunter's conditioning program, as the benefits are numerous. It increases the strength and tone of the hips, stomach, thighs and calves, and improves breathing and stamina. You should use a good-quality jump rope with ball bearing handles made of leather.

Campbell believes there is no substitute for *pushups*, even if you have to begin by doing pushups on your hands and knees, gradually increasing your strength to do a traditional pushup. The benefit of the pushup is to increase your upper body strength. You must be strong in the upper body for a horseback or backpack hunt.

Bicycling is a great exercise for building up thigh muscles used for going up and down steep hills. Campbell uses an exercise bike with a pressure-adjustable wheel, speedometer and odometer.

Campbell considers *walking* better than jogging, since it does not cause stress to the skeletal system, kidneys and other organs. If you will be taking a backpack hunt, you should walk with a loaded backpack. The extra weight will add the desired strength with less distance required. Also, wear your hunting boots when walking, as this conditions the feet to the boot and breaks in boots before the hunt. Jogging is a substitute for walking for those who already jog.

Climbing stairs is Campbell's exercise of choice for an occasional break in the routine, and he recommends it to those who cannot master jumping rope.

Jumping rope gets your heart and lungs in shape, and also strengthens both your upper and lower body, in preparation for a big bear hunt.

Conditioning Program

Here is a good 12-week conditioning program that will prepare you for most big bear hunting. You may need to begin at a different level and increase at a faster or slower pace, according to your ability and physical condition. Twelve weeks is generally ample time to get into shape, but it does not hurt to start earlier, then maintain or even increase your ability and stamina in the final weeks before the hunt.

The activities listed are for every other day. Walk or hike on the "off" days starting at week 5.

Week 1: 100 rope jumps; 15 pushups (five before jumping rope, five after each 50 jumps); one-half mile on the bicycle.

Week 2: 150 rope jumps; 20 pushups (five before jumping rope, five after each 50 jumps); one mile on the bicycle.

Week 3: 200 rope jumps; 25 pushups; one mile on the bicycle.

Week 4: 250 rope jumps; 30 pushups; two miles on the bicycle.

Week 5: 300 rope jumps; 35 pushups; two miles on the bicycle. Add a one-mile walk on off days.

Week 6: 350 rope jumps; 40 pushups; three miles on the bicycle; one-mile walk every other day.

Week 7: 400 rope jumps; 45 pushups; three miles on the bicycle; one-mile walk with backpack every other day.

Week 8: 450 rope jumps; 50 pushups; three miles on the bicycle; one-mile walk with pack every other day.

Week 9: 500 rope jumps; 55 pushups; three miles on the bicycle; one-mile walk with pack every other day.

Week 10: 550 rope jumps; 60 pushups; three miles on the bicycle; two-mile walk with pack every other day.

Week 11: 600 rope jumps; 65 pushups; four miles on the bicycle; two-mile walk with pack every other day.

Week 12: 650 rope jumps; 70 pushups; four miles on the bicycle; two- or three-mile walk with pack every other day.

Getting Started

When to begin your exercise program is of great importance. Campbell begins as far as six months in advance of the hunt, but three months will generally be sufficient unless you are very overweight. If you are overweight, you should begin dieting six months or more in advance, depending upon the amount of weight to be lost.

Start your conditioning program very slowly, especially if you are overweight or have a medical condition that warrants extra caution. Depending on your present condition, begin with something you can actually handle, then each week add more repetitions of the exercises you are using. Most people agree that an every-other-day workout is a good program.

Biking builds strong lungs and legs, two necessities for a bear hunter.

Warnings & Tips

- Do not expand your workouts too quickly. If you find that you have moved ahead more than you should have, drop back to your previous level.
- If you miss a workout or two, don't get discouraged; just start back where you left off.
- Divide and space your pushups before, between and after the jumps.
- Wear good-quality jogging shoes when jumping rope. This will save your feet, ankles and shins a lot of wear and tear.
- Campbell recommends that you begin walking or hiking on the off days starting a month after the every-other-day program. Begin slowly on this also. One mile a day for the first couple of weeks should be sufficient. Increase as you feel you can, and don't forget to wear your hunting boots.
- Mix in stair-climbing and/or jogging as you desire and according to your schedule. If you work in or near a building with several flights of stairs, you will have the perfect opportunity before or after work.

Climbing stairs is one of the best workouts for an upcoming bear hunting adventure. Wear a loaded pack during your workout.

MENTAL CONDITIONING

losely associated to physical conditioning for a bear hunt is mental conditioning, or developing the ability to maintain a positive mental attitude throughout the entire hunt.

I have seen many in-shape hunters give up on a hard hunt long before the hunt was over. No matter how good the guide, a hunter with a bad attitude and no willingness to hunt hard, will fail. This can be downright dangerous when hunting bears. Bottom line: Think positively and have confidence in yourself and your guide.

BAD APPLES

Generally speaking, most hunters, when in good physical condition, are also mentally ready for a hard

hunt. But there are some whose bodies are positive but whose minds are negative. The morale of everyone in camp can be diminished by one hunter with a negative attitude who complains constantly about the weather, the food, the number or size of the bears seen or not seen, etc. Unfortunately, some hunters think they should see bears every day and fill their tags on the first day or two.

Look at it this way: If you were reasonably expected to kill a bear so soon, why would the guide have booked you for a 10- to 14-day hunt? If you're going to be complaining and ready to go home after the third day just because you haven't seen bears yet, you should save your money and stay home.

Then there's the hunter who is not up to the hunt physically. He will often develop a negative mental

Conditioning for the Hunt

Don't put yourself in the situation of not being in shape. You won't regret the time you spend working out during the months before your hunt.

The days of anticipation associated with hunting an animal that is potentially dangerous can take its toll on many hunters. They constantly expect a grizzly to come charging out of every alder thicket or into their tent every night. Each day they become more keyed up until they are about to explode. To escape this feeling, they want to stay in the safety of camp, or if they get a chance to shoot, they will forget marksmanship and shot placement, electing to point and pull the trigger just to get it over with.

attitude early in the hunt. He is embarrassed by not being able to keep up the pace, he feels bad all the time, and he may feel guilty for having spent the family's vacation money for a hunt he's not up to.

OTHER PROBLEMS

Other reasons I have noticed that put hunters in a negative frame of mind include the vastness of the wilderness in which bear hunting is conducted. It's one thing to see vast, open tundra or thick, alder-covered slopes on television, but something quite different when you are there for the first time. The harsh weather that goes along with a hunt in the Far North often frightens hunters. The primitive living conditions in some base or spike camps causes many modern hunters to feel negatively toward the guide and lose confidence in the hunt. I have seen this happen even in very comfortable camps. To some people, camping is fun until you do it.

Don't let an uncomfortable spike camp spoil the hunt experience. Consider it good story material when you get home.

"BEAR FEVER"

From time to time there is a bear hunter who totally loses his mental control, usually when very close to a bear, and cannot fire his rifle. I have never witnessed this myself, but I have talked to guides who have. Darwin Watson of Christina Falls Outfitters in British Columbia related such a story to me.

Watson took one of his hunters into a spike camp to hunt grizzlies. After a four-hour horseback ride in the rain, they set up camp and proceeded to look for a moose kill where one of Watson's other guides had

successfully gotten a hunter a bull moose. After getting some rather bad directions, Watson and his hunter ended up in some heavily burned timber, not sure where the moose kill was.

Both men had rifles. Because of the continuing rain, both were completely suited in nylon raingear—not exactly a quiet procession. Their intentions were to find the moose kill and check for grizzly sign. Watson knew they were reasonably close. He came to realize just how close when he heard a growl and spotted a large grizzly on a burned log only 8 to 10 paces away. Swinging his rifle up and sighting on the bear's neck, Watson directed his hunter to shoot. The hunter swung his rifle up and froze. Despite Watson's rather frantic pleadings to shoot, the hunter just stood there for 10 seconds or so with the bear roaring in their faces. Then the bear turned and disappeared.

Watson said that the hunter later admitted to being frozen with fright, which, as it turned out, was probably best for all concerned under the circumstances. They did get a similar-looking bear three days later about four miles away.

I have experienced several instances when the shooting was anything but good due to fear and/or excitement. This can be a lot worse than freezing and not shooting at all. Having a bear get away without a shot being fired is far better than having a gut-shot grizzly on one's hands.

REALITY ON BEAR NUMBERS

Second only to poor physical condition, the major cause of a hunter developing a negative attitude toward the hunt is the misconception about the abundance of game in the vast Far North. Books, magazines, TV and movies have led many people to believe that bears exist in large numbers throughout all of the Yukon, British Columbia and Alaska. Nothing could be further from the truth. Bears are usually very difficult to find.

It is not unusual to hunt in this vast country for days on end and not only fail to find bears, but fail to see any other game animals either. After a few days of this, many hunters think they've been had by their guide. They give up mentally and cease to hunt hard. They forget that the name of their sport is "hunting," and that means right up until the last moment.

I can't count how many really good bears I've heard about that were taken on the last day of a 10- or 14-day hunt. In many cases, it was the only bear seen. Don't go on a bear hunt expecting to see lots of bears; chances are good that you won't. Be prepared to hunt just as hard the last day with the enthusiasm you had on the first day. This brings about success.

A TOUGH HUNT

A bear hunt is tough and usually physically demanding beyond your expectations. The weather can be rotten for days. The days are long and the nights short. The camps can be somewhat primitive, and the land is vast and can be hostile.

Expect bad weather during your bear hunt and go prepared. It's all part of the fun. You'll be home soon enough.

Big bears are hard to find and are usually few in number. The chances are greater that you will get your bear on the last day of the hunt rather than on the first day. These hunts are expensive, and you may go home without a bear. If you can accept these facts, keeping a positive mental attitude and a high level of confidence and enthusiasm throughout the hunt, then you will make a good bear hunter. If, when you're being honest with yourself, you know your personality or disposition clashes with any of these factors, you may want to consider something other than bear hunting.

Chapter Four

GEARING UP

Y ou won't be going hunting for big bears in your blue jeans, flannel shirt, chukka boots and baseball cap. Bear country is as big and mean and nasty and unforgiving as its clawed inhabitants, and you'd better be dressed right—from the skin out—if you expect to hunt intensely. And don't scrimp on sleeping gear: A well-rested hunter is a sharp-eyed hunter with a good attitude. Here's what to get, and pack.

THE LAYERING CONCEPT

The best way to dress for a cold day of bear hunting is by wearing layers of clothing that provide both insulation and ventilation. As opposed to wearing one very heavy garment, wearing several layers of clothing preserves your body heat while allowing body moisture to evaporate freely.

Another benefit of the layering system is that as the weather changes and you become warmer or colder, layers can be removed or added. The layering concept has been practiced by outdoorsmen for hundreds of years, but today we have garments that make it perform at its best.

The first layer is the "skin layer"—underwear. Underwear provides next-to-the-skin comfort and should be able to "breathe," allowing moisture to escape. Silk or polypropylene are the best materials. This process of breathing wicks moisture away from the skin to the outer layers of clothing. Socks are also part of the skin layer and provide the same function.

The second layer is the inner insulating layer and should be made of loose-fitting layers of shirts, pants, sweaters, vests, boots and insulated pants. When worn loosely, the clothes in this layer can breathe to further expel moisture. On warm, dry days, this could be the final layer.

The third layer is the outer insulating layer, and its job is to protect your body with an insulation that stops the chill of wind and penetrating cold. This layer can also serve as a protective layer, shielding the wearer from rain, snow, briers and brush. This layer is composed of jackets, parkas, hats, gloves, insulated coveralls, etc. This is often the final layer needed.

The fourth layer is the special protective layer. For bear hunting, it may consist of a rainsuit, hip boots or other items to fulfill a special need.

SKIN LAYER

The layer of clothing next to your skin is extremely important, especially in cold weather. During warm, dry weather, cotton or ordinary synthetic underwear and socks will not get you into trouble; however, in weather that is wet and/or cold, as you will generally encounter on big bear hunts, you have a different and often dangerous situation.

UNDERWEAR

When it's wet, cotton or cotton/polyester underwear loses its insulating value and increases the rate at which the body loses its heat.

For many years the outdoorsman's only effective choice of long underwear for cold weather was wool or two-layered underwear made of cotton on the inside and wool on the outside. However, thanks to high-tech breakthroughs in man-made fabrics, today there are some other choices in underwear for wet and/or cold weather that give the wearer maximum protection.

Polypropylene

The first man-made fabric to enter the underwear market with very positive results was polypropylene. This nonabsorbent, soft, stretchable, body-hugging fabric wicks moisture away from the skin, yet it stops the movement of air on the skin's surface, resulting in a retention of body heat.

An effective use of polypropylene is in medium-weight underwear for active outdoorsmen, a two-layered garment that combines 53 percent soft wool with 47 percent polypropylene. The polypropylene is the inner layer and the wool is the outer. This combination allows moisture to be wicked away from the skin to the outer wool layer where the moisture evaporates. This keeps the layer next to the skin dry. Add to that the insulating value of the wool, and you have warmth in very cold weather.

Thermax

One of the most effective underwear fabrics for cold or wet weather is DuPont's Thermax. It is made from a unique hollow fiber, which has been designed to give the wearer the softness of cotton, but with wicking ability to pull moisture away from the body for evaporation.

The hollow fiber used in the construction of the fabric also maximizes the amount of entrapped air to provide superior insulating capabilities, a critical factor for warmth. Thermax is easy to care for, as it retains its shape and resists shrinkage when laundered. It is also resistant to mildew and doesn't retain odor.

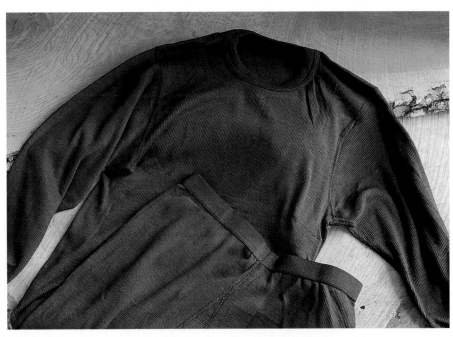

Wet, cold weather comes with big bear hunting. A clothing layer next to your skin that wicks moisture away from your body will keep you warm and comfortable; polypropylene (shown), Thermax and other fabrics do the job.

Other Fabrics

Capilene and CoolMax are other synthetic underwear fabrics that aggressively wick moisture off the skin, dry rapidly and provide insulation. They come in lightweight, middleweight and expedition or BiPolar weight sizes; choose a weight depending on time of year and anticipated worst-case weather. Use tops that have a zippered neck, which makes venting easy during strenuous hiking and climbing.

SOCKS

Socks are an essential part of the skin layer. Like underwear, their comfort and wicking ability plays a

Good socks will wick moisture away from your skin yet not restrict blood flow to your feet.

major role in keeping the wearer warm.

The part of us that seems to get cold first is the feet, and with good reason. Our body is programmed to automatically regulate its warmth requirements for survival. In cold conditions, the brain and central nervous system receive the highest priority. In order to keep these vital areas warm, circulation to the extremities is curtailed. Since our feet are the farthest distance from the core, they are the first to feel the reduced circulation. *Voila*, you have cold feet.

Double Up & Other Sock Secrets

Cold weather foot covering should start with two pairs of socks. Since the feet are active sweat producers, the socks next to your skin should be made of polypropylene, Thermax or other modern, synthetic wicking fabric for the same reasons these materials make great underwear.

The outer socks should be wool or wool-blend. Don't wear socks that are too thick, as they can cut off circulation when wedged between the foot and a tight-fitting boot. Make sure your wool sock is high enough to come up above the top of the boot. This can keep it from slipping down into the boot and cutting off circulation.

Before you put on your boots, make sure all wrinkles are smoothed out of your socks. Wrinkled socks are not only uncomfortable, but they also slow down the blood circulation to the feet and toes and can cause blisters.

As a bear hunter, you're likely to do a great deal of walking and will frequently be in wet conditions, so carry an extra pair of liner socks and wool socks in your daypack. Change socks when your feet become damp and cold, and you'll feel like a new person, ready to find the big bear around the next hill.

Underwear Facts

Here are some points to consider when buying underwear for cold weather:

• Purchase wool, cotton or wool/cotton blend underwear one size larger, as some shrinkage will occur.

• When selecting two-piece long underwear, be sure the top half is long enough to fit well down into the lower half. Exposed bare skin in the kidney area can chill the wearer and offset the underwear's value.

• Don't buy underwear with legs that are too long for you. Long legs may bunch up in the boot, cutting off circulation and resulting in cold feet.

• Follow the laundering instructions to the letter. Wool can shrink to the point of looking like it was made for a child. Polypropylene, as well as many other synthetics, is sensitive to heat, and excessive heat may ruin its shape.

THE INNER INSULATING LAYER

The second layer of clothing is one which the wearer can tailor to fit the circumstances of the hunt. In cool weather, the shirt may be of chamois or corduroy, worn with lightweight cotton duck pants or denim jeans.

But you must be prepared for worse conditons! When the weather gets cold, this layer must be taken more seriously.

UPPER BODY: INSULATE & VENTILATE

In cold weather, the upper part of the inner insulating layer must serve several purposes. It must first insulate. Secondly, it must be capable of ventilating.

In order to carry out these functions, it is best if several layers are worn.

Let's say that on an early-morning, late-spring bear hunt, you know that it's going to be about 20ºF for the first few hours, but later on during the day you expect temperatures in the 40s. Over your underwear you may wear a long-sleeved cotton-blend shirt, with a wool sweater over that. If the day does in fact warm up, you can pull off the sweater and store it in your daypack.

Strategies & Fabrics

These inner layers can be made up of shirts,

       Gearing Up

Because they're warm and quiet, wool pants should be the official pants of big bear hunters. Consider cuffless pants to avoid collecting snow and woods trash.

moving around.

- Shirts should have long tails that will stay inside the trousers, even after a long day of climbing over obstacles, to protect the kidney area.

If cold and wet conditions are expected, a shirt made of wool blend will be a good choice, as wool is not only warm, but resistant to moisture and warm even when wet. Wool also breathes, allowing body vapor to evaporate. Finally, wool is superior in quietness, which is important in any stalk (if this layer becomes your outer layer).

LOWER BODY: PANTS FACTS

The second part of the outer insulating layer is the pants. First of all, the pants selected should not be too tight around the waist. When trying on pants, remember to leave a little room for long underwear. The belt loops should be wide enough to accommodate your hunting belt. The pants should be cuffless, as cuffs are collection points for sticks, leaves, pebbles, snow, and so on. Wool and other heavy pants should have buttons for attaching suspenders.

When purchasing pants for bear hunting, keep in mind the conditions under which you will be using them. Will you need wool for snow and damp cold? Will you be hunting in thick brush, briers or rocks, where tough Cordura fabric or nylon-faced pants will be needed? The answers to these questions will help you select the proper hunting pants. Also, your guide can help you make a wise selection.

sweaters and vests. The number and weight are choices that only you can make based on your own comfort requirements, but here are a few principles to remember:

- All layers should be from medium- to lightweight.
- It is better to have two or three layers than to have one heavy shirt.
- These layers should not be so bulky that they make movement difficult.
- Layers should fit loosely so that you get a bellows effect to facilitate ventilation when

Pants Fabrics

Pants can be either a fleece material—Polarfleece, PolarTec, Browning Hydro-Fleece and the like—or wool, again depending on the season. Fleece dries quickly, breathes well and keeps its insulation value when wet, as does wool, which doesn't dry quite as quickly. Regardless, the pants must have wide belt loops, zipper front and at least two deep front pockets and one deep rear pocket.

Suspenders allow you to wear your belt loose, and help keep you warm by not restricting blood circulation to the lower extremities.

Suspenders & Belts

How you hold your pants up is important during cold weather. A surprising number of people hunting during cold weather have cold feet and legs due, in part, to the fact they have their belt too tight. This not only restricts circulation, causing the extremities to get cold, it also stops ventilation, which adds to the problem. A good pair of suspenders can go a long way toward keeping you warm. Outdoorsmen in colder climates have known this for centuries.

Even with suspenders, a belt is an important item of equipment because it is where items such as knife sheaths, cartridge holders and mini-flashlight holders are worn. Belts are also needed if hip boots or brush chaps are worn, as these items are attached to the belt. Your belt should be of good quality and not rolled over around the edges. Elastic belts and narrow ones are inappropriate for hunters.

TAKE CARE OF YOUR FEET

One of the single most important items in the layering system is included in this outer insulating layer: footwear. No bear hunter can do his or her best with tired, hurting or cold feet. Since most bear hunting trips include a lot of walking, good footwear is important to the well-being of the hunter and to the enjoyment of the hunt.

It wasn't too long ago that hunting boots were little more than work boots or military surplus boots in a different box. However, thanks to modern technology and materials, this has changed, and now there are lightweight boots available for hunting that can also keep your feet dry and warm.

Boot Materials

In the past, leather was the only quality material of which boots were made. But leather has been joined by man-made materials that provide many of the same advantages. DuPont's Cordura nylon has enabled boot and shoe manufacturers to make rugged footwear that is lightweight. Some boots weigh half as much as they did when they were all leather. Also, boots made with Cordura may come in a camouflage pattern, and they are quick to dry. Cordura is strong and abrasion-resistant. Several boot companies use Cordura and leather as the outer layer of hunting boots with a full-sock Gore-Tex inner lining for waterproofing. Thinsulate is also being used as insulation for warmth.

Hunters have never had a better selection of boots than they do today. Carefully match your boots to the conditions where you plan to hunt.

Sole Considerations

The soles of boots have changed a great deal as well. Several years ago the choices in soles were slim, usually either heavy lugged soles or smooth soles. Now there is a wide variety of soles that range between these extremes. The new soles are lighter and more flexible.

For bear hunting in rough areas during all types of weather, a waterproof, all-leather or Cordura/leather combination boot 10 to 12 inches high would be a good choice. The type of sole selected should be given some thought and matched to the terrain most likely to be encountered. A deep-treaded sole is excellent for climbing rocky mountains but can add pounds to your feet if worn in a muddy area.

Important Boot Notes

Whether to purchase insulated or uninsulated boots is a factor to be considered. If most of your hunting is done during warmer months, the need for insulation may not be great.

If you elect to purchase some of the high-quality

Opt for today's light, flexible (but still tough) soles. Take pains to make sure your boots fit perfectly ... and then break them in gently but completely before you hunt.

leather boots found on today's market, be sure you learn to care for them properly. Get a good supply of a wax compound such as Sno-Seal and coat the boots regularly according to directions.

For wet conditions, the popular leather or Cordura top and rubber-bottomed "pacs" are often a good choice. Many of these boots are waterproof and may be purchased with insulated liners, which make them good for use in very cold weather and in snow. If you purchase these boots with a removable insulating liner, be sure to buy extra liners to have along when your main ones get wet!

Regardless of which type of shoe or boot you select, be sure to take your time in getting fitted. Wear the same sock combination to the store that you plan to wear with the boots in the field. Make sure that the footwear is not too tight with that sock combination. Purchase an extra set of laces when you buy your footwear and keep the laces in your daypack. Be sure to get complete instructions on how to properly care for your new footwear.

When wearing your boots in cold weather, remember not to lace them tightly. This can reduce blood circulation and cause cold feet. Many seasoned hunters buy their cold weather boots one full size larger than normal to leave room for two pairs of socks.

For wet conditions consider combination boots. Insulated inserts may be necessary for hunts in snow.

THE OUTER INSULATING LAYER

CAPS & HATS

The first item to consider for the outer layer is a cap or hat. During warm weather, a baseball-style cap goes a long way toward keeping the head shaded and cool. However, as the weather cools down, much more serious consideration needs to be given to the head gear. A tremendous amount of the body's total heat production may be lost through an unprotected head.

For cool days when hunting in high open country, a beaver-felt, western-style hat will conserve heat and protect the head from bright sun, rain, hail or sleet. In other areas, the hunter may want to wear a Jones-style hat or baseball-style cap that is insulated.

Make sure the cap you choose can be pulled down to give your ears protection.

Head off the Cold

If the weather is cold, many hunters want maximum protection. This is provided by a knit cap called a balaclava, or snow or tundra mask. It can be worn rolled up as a knit cap. When the weather gets colder, it can be rolled down to serve as a face mask, giving protection to the head, face and neck.

At one time, the best balaclavas were made of wool and were uncomfortable to many people when worn next to the skin. Now balaclavas are available with a wool outer layer and polypropylene inner

A well insulated, waterproof, quiet jacket should be high on the list of every bear hunter. Bear hunting weather often changes by the hour.

ered it can warm other parts of the body. The mountain men had a saying, "When your feet are cold, put on your hat." It makes sense.

COATS, JACKETS & OVERALLS

The second item in this layer is the coat, jacket, parka or coveralls you will wear. Obviously, if the weather is warm, you may not need a coat of any type. However, if your hunt takes you into the really cold country where rain or snow is likely, you need to know something about insulation and fabrics.

If you think the choice of insulation is somewhat confusing, you'll be dazzled by the choice of fabrics your outer garments may be made from. There are almost as many different fabrics as there are manufacturers. You'll find that many of these are waterproof, silent in brush, tough to tear, easy to clean and long-lasting under hunting conditions.

The first rule to follow when purchasing a hunting coat, parka or jacket is to buy from a reputable dealer who handles brand-name equipment. High-quality insulated hunting garments are not cheap, but they are long-lasting and worth the cost. Your life may depend on it, and you can bet your hunting success will.

Always bring a jacket. It should be made of either fleece or one of the new burr-proof outer fabrics like Saddle Cloth, Stealth Cloth, Ambush Cloth, Cabela's Burr Barrier, Browning Hydro-Fleece, Whitewater Outdoors Arctic Fleece, or 10X ShikariCloth, preferably with either Gore Windstopper or a Gore-Tex laminate. These jackets are warm but not heavy or bulky, quiet and almost impossible to rip. The Gore laminates make them 100 percent windproof, and a Gore-Tex laminate adds waterproofness. A lightweight, packable Gore-Tex rain suit fits into a small stuff-sack and will double as a wind shell.

Some companies offer matching insulated trousers to go with their insulated hunting coats. These are

layer. The polypropylene is comfortable next to the skin and does a good job of wicking moisture away from the head.

When it is windy or raining, the balaclava will not be enough. At this time, an insulated hood on a coat or parka will be needed, or at least a rainsuit with a hood.

If weather is uncertain, a balaclava can be carried in the daypack and a cooler hat worn. Since the head is a principal point of heat loss, when properly cov-

especially useful to those who hunt bears from blinds or use boats for transportation.

GLOVES

The last item in this layer is by far not the least in importance—gloves. In cold climates, the bare hand holding a bow, rifle or handgun is losing heat to the cold object. If a hunter has on gloves of poor quality and the gloves are wet, he loses further heat to the cold. A good pair of gloves can prevent this heat loss and help keep the hunter warm.

Today there is no reason for a hunter to suffer from cold, wet hands. The hunting equipment industry has made great strides in handwear, and anyone who can afford a big bear hunt can certainly afford the outstanding gloves available on the market.

The first thing that strikes the shopper looking for a new pair of gloves is the vast array of gloves now available for hunting. There are gloves for cold, wet conditions, gloves for use with horses, gloves for keeping the stand-hunter's hands warm, camouflage gloves, blaze-orange gloves, white gloves, mittens with a shooting finger and many more special-use gloves.

Get the Right Material

All gloves are not for all purposes. Bear hunters who hunt in wet conditions should consider insulated gloves made from Gore-Tex. Gore-Tex will keep wetness out, yet permit the perspiration of the hand to escape, thus assuring your hands of dry warmth.

The drawback of many gloves made of insulation and/or Gore-Tex, as well as other materials, is that the trigger finger may be so thick that it will not fit into the trigger guard, or if it does, the fit is so tight as to inadvertently pull the trigger. All gloves should be tested for ease of trigger control *before* purchasing.

Leather gloves made from deerskin or cowhide offer the wearer a firm grip and protection from rough surfaces. These are the preferred gloves by many who hunt on horseback. Gloves made from soft cowhide or deerskin are supple and give a shooter the feel he needs when handling his firearm.

The drawbacks to leather gloves are twofold. First, they do not retain your body heat unless they are lined with some type of insulation or an insulation insert is worn under them. Second, leather gets wet

quickly and is slow to dry. If such gloves are not dried slowly, they can become stiff.

Wool gloves were once the standby for hunters in cold weather; however, they must have a waterproof and windproof outer shell in order to keep a hunter's hands warm in cold, windy or wet conditions.

Gloves are available with nylon shells and down as insulation. These work okay when dry; once wet, down insulation is useless.

When purchasing gloves, make sure they are a good fit. They should not be so tight as to cut off circulation in the fingers or compress the insulation. Both of these conditions can cause very cold fingers. Likewise, avoid gloves that are so loose they hamper your sense of touch.

Cold, wet hands can ruin a day of hunting. A high-quality pair of gloves in your daypack can make the difference.

SPECIAL PROTECTIVE LAYERS

*T*here are times when the hats, coats, pants and boots of the outer insulating layer aren't enough. Many special situations call for special gear suited to the weather or hunting technique that is needed to get you your bear. For instance, wading creeks for brown bears or hunting mountain grizzlies in a downpour calls for a special protective layer of clothing.

RAINGEAR

The most often-used protective clothing for bear hunters is raingear, and there is perhaps no item of clothing which has improved as much over the years. There once was a time when waterproof raingear—the kind that wouldn't leak even in a prolonged downpour—was so tight that the wearer could get

just as wet on the inside from moisture released by the body: The raingear didn't breathe. This has changed, and there are several new materials on the market which can keep the wearer dry from the outside and on the inside.

Perhaps the best known of the truly waterproof fabrics is still Gore-Tex. The key to the waterproof, windproof, breathable performance of Gore-Tex fabric lies in the patented microporous Gore-Tex membrane which is laminated to outer shell fabrics. The Gore-Tex membrane contains 9 billion pores per

Above: Expect rain on a bear hunt. Get the best raingear you can afford and pack it in your daypack. Left: Be prepared for dealing with water other than rain. Ask your guide whether you should bring hip boots.

square inch, each 20,000 times smaller than a water drop, but 700 times larger than a water vapor molecule. The membrane, therefore, effectively blocks wind and weather but allows moisture from perspiration to escape.

Helping Your Clothes Perform

After you have gone to great care and expense to purchase the right kinds of clothing for your bear hunt, there are a few simple measures you can take to help them perform at their best.

You should never sleep in the clothes you wear during the day. Most experienced outdoorsmen sleep in the nude. This allows their clothes to air out and keeps their clothes from absorbing moisture from the body during the night. You should also air your sleeping bag daily.

Carry along a few high-energy food bars or non-melting chocolate candy in your daypack or hunting coat pocket to nibble on during the day. Carbohydrates can provide the body with inner warmth and energy needed in cold climates.

The most important thing you can do is try to avoid sweating. Make sure your clothing is loose-fitting, and as you get warm from activity or rising temperatures, begin opening or removing layers.

HIP BOOTS

More often than not, the grizzly hunter will find that hip boots will be a required item on his what-to-bring list. This is one more item that should be selected with extreme care. Cheap, poorly selected hip boots can almost ruin your feet within a few hours and bring your hunt to a stop.

Tips for Shopping Carefully

The first step in buying hip boots is to take your time when shopping. Wear the same type clothing and socks you plan to wear when bear hunting. Try on and test-walk a variety of hip boots to find which ones fit you best. I find that hip boots generally run larger in size than my leather boots. For example, I normally wear a size 12 boot, but my hip boot size is usually 11, even with heavy socks.

On the other hand, be careful not to buy hip boots that are too tight. Try them out thoroughly before making a decision. Stick with well-known brand names and buy the very best you can afford.

Avoid stocking-foot hip boots and get boot-foot hip boots. The boot-foot wader will give you a firmer footing and will protect your shins during inevitable stumbles over logs and stumps. The heavier material will resist snagging, and you won't have to pack along the wading boots that stocking-foot hippers require.

When buying hip boots, be sure to get the simple repair kit that comes with most. High-quality hip boots are virtually puncture-proof with normal wear, but a repair kit is a good item to have on a remote bear hunt.

COMFORTABLE SLEEPING GEAR

Selecting a sleeping bag and pad for bear hunting camp should be done with great care, as this is the key to a good night's sleep, which is essential to good hunting. Do not take this lightly! Your hunt's success may depend on it. And besides, it is an investment that should last for years.

INSULATION CONSIDERATIONS

The first thing to look for in a sleeping bag is the degree of warmth it offers. A sleeping bag keeps you warm by retaining the heat generated by your body. The holding in of this heat is made possible by the insulation with which the bag has been filled. The key element to insulation is loft, or dead air space in the insulating material. The thicker the loft, the warmer the bag.

The best-known insulating fillers used in high-quality sleeping bags are down, PolarGuard, Dacron Hollofil and Quallofil. Since grizzly hunting is often done in wet conditions, I have retired my down bag for this sport and depend upon the man-made fillers which still insulate when damp. Many hunters have replaced their down bags with Quallofil bags due to its compactibility, a real plus when packing space is limited.

BAG SHAPE

The shape of your sleeping bag is something you must consider when shopping. Most sleeping bags come in one of three shapes—mummy, taper or rectangular. The mummy bag fits snugly around your body and usually has a head and neck closure for extra warmth. They usually weigh less due to their size, but offer maximum warmth. This type of bag is best for backpacking or extremely cold conditions.

The taper bag does not fit as tightly around the body as does the mummy bag, but it offers more freedom of movement and packs into a small space.

The rectangular bag offers the user plenty of room for stretching and turning during the night. These bags usually don't have a hood. Also, they weigh more than the mummy or taper bag and take up more packing space. You might choose a rectangular bag when space and weight are not considerations. They are very comfortable bags to use in a base camp.

FOUR RULES

Since sleeping bag construction varies greatly among manufacturers, *rule number one* for buying sleeping bags is to buy from a reputable dealer who handles brand-name equipment. Bargain hunting can be a mistake.

Rule number two: Decide how much insulation you need for your bear camp. This varies from person to person. If your camping is mostly done during cool to cold months, as most bear hunts are, you need a bag that will allow you to sleep comfortably at low temperatures. The best solution is to rent a quality sleeping bag and use it on a cold weather camping trip; test insulation levels before buying.

Rule number three: Don't let someone talk you into a backpack bag or mummy bag unless you need lightweight camping gear. I find that I sleep much more comfortably in a full-size sleeping bag that has

A good night's sleep can spell success. A full-sized self-inflating foam pad makes a comfortable camp bed. (Don't forget to pack a patch kit.)

a zipper across the lower end and up one side. On warm nights, I leave the bag unzipped and pull the top over me as the night cools. The full-size bag also gives me more room for moving my legs.

Rule number four: Once you get a good sleeping bag, take care of it. Make it a daily practice to air it when in camp. This airing will help eliminate moisture build-up, a common occurrence on many camping trips, as well as restore loft to the insulation.

SLEEPING PAD

You will want to go one step further to ensure your nights afield are restful: buy a good sleeping pad to go under the bag. While you are sleeping in your bag, the portion underneath you becomes temporarily compressed, allowing body heat to escape. This heat loss can be acute if air is permitted to circulate under the bag, as when sleeping on a canvas cot. Many air mattresses and foam pads are available today, but the type that I have found to give the most dependable service is a self-inflating foam pad.

Be sure to get a full-sized pad so that your entire body is comfortable. These pads are a combination of an airtight, waterproof nylon skin bonded to an open-cell foam. When inflated, air is trapped within the foam pad. When you lie on the pad, your weight pressurizes the trapped air. The pressurized air supports you off the ground and minimizes foam compression under your hips and shoulders. It can make a cold spike camp feel like a Hilton!

The pressurized air also maximizes foam loft for greatest insulation. Unlike air mattresses, which

You can stay warm and comfortable when you're cold-weather hunting for either polar bears or grizzlies if you plan ahead and pack for the cold. Very few bears are taken by the campfire.

have no insulation, these pads have four times the insulation of the closed-cell foam pads used by many backpackers.

If you are accustomed to sleeping on a pillow, take an inflatable or compressible foam pillow on your bear hunt with you. I have seen many otherwise properly equipped hunters sleep poorly from not having a comfortable pillow. Sound, restful sleep is important on a bear hunt. If you don't feel good because of bad sleep, you won't hunt well.

Gearing Up

OTHER IMPORTANT GEAR

have good light-gathering capability and are usually lightweight, weighing about 1¼ pound.

Choosing Binoculars

Other features on binoculars are very much a personal choice. For bear hunting, the magnification should be from 7 to 9 power. Whether your binoculars have center focus adjustment or individual eyepiece adjustment is up to you.

The best guide to selecting binoculars is to stay with the well-known brand names and get the best you can afford. Before making a final selection, go to your sporting goods dealer and take the time to handle a number of binoculars. Don't rush into a decision. Get binoculars that are comfortable to wear around your neck and tucked inside your jacket. Purchase a better strap if needed! Get binoculars that you can easily adjust to your eyes and that will *stay* adjusted. Make sure the image is bright and clear and sharp.

BINOCULARS

Long hours spent glassing valleys, mountain slopes and beaches are a major part of any bear hunt, and one of the most-used items on these hunts is a good pair of binoculars. This is not the piece of equipment to try to save a few dollars on, as cheap optics can make a day of glassing miserable, with much of the day and all of the evening spent nursing a headache.

Since most bear hunts involve a lot of walking and sometimes climbing over rocks or through timber, medium-sized binoculars are usually the best choice. Compact binoculars have a small objective lens, making their use limited in low-light conditions. In addition, prolonged use can cause eyestrain.

The large objective lens binoculars, while having good light-gathering capability, are large in body size and often heavy, making them hard to hold still (which will also cause eyestrain). Thus the reason for the mid-size binoculars, such as 7x30 or 9x35. They

DAYPACK

Your daypack for bear hunting should be larger than the cheaper models that are sold for carrying schoolbooks. Remember, you want enough room to store clothing you've shed as well as carry other essential items.

The daypack should be made from a strong material that is quiet and not scratchy-loud. It should also have padded shoulder straps for comfortable carrying and one or more outside pockets that are easy to access for such items as a canteen, binoculars, trail snacks or map; this is much quicker and easier than having to dig through the main compartment where

Test binoculars before you buy them and choose only those that offer excellent viewing in low-light conditions. Bear hunting is often best just before dark, or in dark forests.

many items may be. It is also convenient to have a reinforced tie-on accessory patch. With these patches you can roll up a sweater or coat and tie it onto the outside of the pack.

DUFFELS

Many duffel bags are available to the hunter today, but the best I have found, in size, shape and durability, is a surplus U.S. Air Force Cargo Kit Bag that measures 23-by-15-by-13 inches. I can get everything in it for a two-week grizzly hunt with the exception of my firearm and camera gear. I stress this because many hunters bring *too much* gear.

If your guide uses a Super Cub to get you into camp, chances are that he will restrict your gear to 40 pounds, and I have hunted with outfitters who used boats who also had a 40-pound restriction.

TALK TO THE EXPERTS

Before you start shopping for clothing or camping gear I suggest that you talk to your guide or outfitter and get his opinion on what and how much you need. The Big bear country is giant in size, and what works on Kodiak Island may not be a good idea in the Cassiar Mountains of British Columbia. Most guides and outfitters have a good idea of exactly what you

need to bring with you and will send you a checklist for packing.

This is especially true for polar bear hunts where much of the gear is highly specialized and may be rented or furnished by the outfitter or guide.

FINAL GEAR NOTES

In closing this chapter, I encourage you to purchase your bear hunting clothing and gear early and become familiar with its use before you show up in bear camp. When I was guiding, nothing predicted the failure of a hunt quicker than a hunter arriving in camp wearing new boots and cutting tags off his gear as he unpacked. We usually wound up wasting hunting time showing him how to lay out his camp bed, put on his new underwear, try to stretch his undersize new cap and treat the blisters on his feet.

Use your equipment often enough to know how to use it properly when you reach bear camp, and have your boots well broken in. Take the same pride in your personal gear as you do your rifle and load. Your hunt will go better and be a lot more fun if you do.

Being properly dressed and having the right sleeping gear for the weather conditions can be as critical to a bear hunt as having the right rifle and ammunition. It can mean the difference between success and failure, enjoyment and misery, and possibly, life and death. It's not cheap, but neither is a big bear hunt.

The serious bear hunter will spend long hours away from the camp. Your daypack will be your lifeline to comfort and safety.

Gearing Up

Chapter Five

BIG BEARS, BIG GUNS

Y ou've planned as deeply as a person can plan. Bought the best gear. Worked yourself into physical and mental toughness. Dreamed. Flown a few thousand miles, hopped on a puddle jumper, ridden a boat. Hunted for six days straight. Walked more than a hundred miles. Seen one bear a half-mile off. And you're on one—now! After a five-minute run to a ridge he's there, 121 yards away. It all comes down to this—one shot that you better make good on—for the success of your hunt, maybe even for your own safety. Here's how to ensure the outcome is the one you want.

CARTRIDGES &
CALIBERS FOR BIG BEARS

Putting a grizzly, brown or polar bear down for keeps is no easy task. It has been well documented since Europeans in North America first encountered grizzlies that a lot of gun, combined with good marksmanship, is required, especially if the bear is excited. Same goes for browns and polars.

BIG BEARS WERE MEAN THEN ...

One of the first big bears spotted by the Lewis and Clark Expedition was a large grizzly lying on a ridge some 300 yards from the Missouri River. Six of the expedition's best hunters slipped to within 40 yards of the bear. Four of the hunters shot their muzzle-loading rifles at the bear, while two held their fire—

just in case.

When the four shots were fired, two of the balls went all the way through the bear, penetrating both lungs, but the enraged bear jumped to its feet and charged the group. The two hunters who had held their fire now shot, breaking one of the bear's shoulders. Still the charge continued, straight toward the two hunters who had shot last. These two hunters dropped their rifles and raced to the river, diving off a 20-foot bluff into the water. The bear followed on their heels, splashing heavily into the murky, brown water.

The first hunters to shoot had now reloaded, and shooting from the top of the bluff, finally put a ball through the grizzly's head. When the bear was butchered, the hunters found that eight balls had passed through its body in various directions.

... AND THEY'RE MEAN NOW

Even during modern times when rifles producing high velocities and high energy levels are used, every hunting season we hear stories of grizzlies taking a solid hit, then getting away, or worse yet, charging hunters.

In one such case, a guide had booked a pair of hunters on a combination moose and grizzly hunt. All three had rifles chambered in .300 Win. Mag. On the third morning of the hunt, the guide took the hunters to a moose carcass where a grizzly had reportedly been feeding.

When the trio got within 50 yards of the carcass, the bear, standing on a log near the bait, looked straight at them. Even with the wind in their favor, the bear had caught their scent and held his head high, trying to get a better fix on the human smell. The guide whispered to one of the hunters to get a rest and shoot. At the report of the rifle, the bear was knocked off the log and turned flips in the snow.

"Shoot again," the guide instructed the hunter. He did, but hit the left front leg. At this shot, the bear headed for the hunters.

By now, everyone was shooting. The guide put a shot into the bear's chest, and the two hunters emptied their rifles, hitting the animal at least five times in the face and throat area. Only once during those terrifying seconds did the bear lose his footing.

Still charging, the bear reached the trio. One hunter ran to the left, the other to the right, both trying to reload. The guide jumped behind a large tree, but the bear had a fix on him and was there in a second. The bear's first blow sent the guide's rifle flying and knocked the man down. Next, the bear bit the guide's left arm and then the top of his head, literally scalping him.

The two hunters had reloaded and were now trying to get a clear shot at the enraged beast. At the first opportunity, both hunters fired simultaneously from 10 feet. The bear fell on the guide. Thinking the bear dead, the hunters ran over and pulled the guide from under the animal, but as they did, the

Use enough rifle to bring a big bear down.

bear bawled and tried to get up. A shot to the bruin's brain finally ended the rage. The guide lived, thanks to some skillful medical attention.

This was not a large coastal brown bear, but a mountain grizzly estimated to weigh 400 pounds. Yet he took all that the .300 Win. Mag. had to offer and still put up a good fight. It takes a lot to put a grizzly down for keeps, and the hunter new to the pursuit of big bears needs to be keenly aware of this.

The objective in big bear hunting must always be to make a clean kill. Nothing is worse than not hitting a bear properly, either with a bad shot or with the wrong gun and load. The mauling of the guide in the previous example was caused when the hunter who fired the first shot with his .300 Win. Mag. hit the bear too far back, missing all the vitals. Many a good man has gone to an early grave because he—or his hunting partner—didn't hit a bear right the first time.

Select a caliber and load that offers enough downrange energy to stop a large bear. The marksmanship is up to you.

SELECTING A CALIBER/LOAD

Making a clean kill on a bear begins with selecting a cartridge/bullet combination that is capable of killing a bear quickly *if* you use good marksmanship. But first, you should know what really puts an animal down when it is struck by a bullet. During my years of guiding hunters, I found that many hunters were knowledgeable of firearms and ballistics, but few knew much about what actually killed an animal when it was hit by a fast-moving projectile.

Big game may be killed by a bullet in a number of ways. For instance, the bullet may strike the heart, cutting off the animal's blood supply. A bullet in the brain stops all vital life support systems. A bullet in the lungs destroys the respiratory system. A wound to the diaphragm, a muscular membrane that aids the lungs in pumping air, can also be deadly after a period of time, as can a wound to the liver. Even a wound to a non-vital area may eventually

lead to death.

With the exception of the spine or brain shot, any of these fatal hits may not knock a big bear down, allowing him to travel some distance before falling—a dangerous situation with a bear. In such cases, the hunter may blame his rifle and cartridge for not having enough "knockdown power."

Go for Shock Power

Another way a bullet can kill a bear and take him off his feet instantly is with shock, more precisely "hydrostatic shock." Shock waves are carried very rapidly at full force by water (of which an animal's body is primarily composed) and break down the solid materials—in this case, the bear's vitals—in the water. It is this shock, caused by the transfer of energy from the bullet into the tissue of the animal, and not the bullet itself, that we know as "knockdown power."

Comparative Rifle Ballistics

Cartridge	Bullet Wt. (Grs.)	Muzzle Velocity (fps)	Muzzle Energy (fp)	Downrange Energy (fp) 100 Yds.	200 Yds.
.338 Win. Mag.	200	2,960	3,892	3,138	2,506
.30-30 Win.	170	2,200	1,827	1,356	990
.35 Rem.	200	2,080	1,922	1,281	841

You can see by this chart that only the .338 Win. Mag. makes the big bear cut of at least 2,000 foot-pounds (Fp) of energy, at both 100 and 200 yards in this case.

When selecting a cartridge, hunters are too often concerned with only the trajectory of their bullet at longer ranges, failing to consider the loss of energy by the bullet and the importance of retaining enough downrange energy to put a big bear down. Anyone hunting big bears should select a caliber/load combination that delivers enough downrange kinetic energy, or "knockdown power," for the extreme range at which a shot may be taken. Ample kinetic energy will break heavy bones, make a sizable wound channel, destroy vital organs and produce immobilizing shock.

Please take note that this is *downrange* energy and not muzzle energy. The difference is great, and too many hunters are only aware of their load's muzzle energy, not the retained energy level where the animal is.

You won't feel the wallop of recoil when you're in the heat of the moment, shooting the bear of a lifetime. But you will feel the pain on the practice range; you have to learn to deal with it.

2,000 Foot-Pounds at 150 Yards

Cartridges and bullet weights that maintain 2,000 foot-pounds of energy with factory loads out to 150 yards (the maximum range for shooting big bears, according to almost every big bear outfitter I've talked to) include:

Cartridge	Bullet Weight (in grains)
.270 Win.	130
.270 Wthby Mag.	130 and 150
.280 Rem.	150 and 165
.284 Win.	150
7mm Rem. Mag.	125, 150 and 175
7mm Wthby Mag.	139, 154 and 175
.30-06	150, 165 and 180
.300 Win. Mag.	150, 180 and 220
.300 H&H Mag.	150, 180 and 220
.300 Wthby Mag.	150 and 180
.300 Rem. Ultra Mag.	180
.30-378 Wthby. Mag.	180 and 220
.308 Win.	180
8mm Rem. Mag.	185 and 220
.338 Win. Mag.	200, 225 and 250
.338 Rem. Ultra Mag.	250
.338-378 Wthby Mag.	200, 225 and 250
.340 Wthby Mag.	200 and 250
.350 Rem. Mag.	200
.375 H&H Mag.	270 and 300
.378 Wthby Mag.	300
.416 Rem. Mag.	350 and 400
.416 Rigby	350 and 400
.416 Wthby Mag.	350 and 400
.458 Win. Mag.	500
.460 Wthby Mag.	500

CARTRIDGE SELECTION

Choose a cartridge with enough powder capacity in the case to push the properly constructed bullet fast enough to get the downrange energy level needed to put a bear down.

While there are no hard-and-fast rules on how much downrange energy is enough for a bear, it is generally accepted that 2,000 foot-pounds is sufficient for bears weighing up to 600 pounds, and 2,800 foot-pounds of energy is needed for bears of more than 600 pounds. This quickly rules out a lot of cartridges. Yes, I know big bears have been taken with such small cartridges as .17 Rem., .22 Hornet, .222 Rem., .223 Rem. and .30-30 Win., but these were exceptions. Who knows how many bears have been wounded by puny cartridges and how many hunters mauled as a result of such a poor choice?

Real-Life Opinions

Ask inexperienced bear hunters to name the best cartridges for hunting big bears and you will hear arguments for everything from the .30-30 Win. on up. Ask the same question of those hunters who have faced big bears, and the minimum caliber usually starts with the .300 Win. Mag.

To hear the opinions of those who face grizzlies regularly, I surveyed many professional grizzly guides in Alaska, the Yukon and British Columbia, asking what rifle caliber they preferred that their hunters use. The .338 Win. Mag. was by far the favorite by both inland and brown bear guides.

A few inland grizzly guides, like Ken Kyllo of Hudson's Hope, British Columia, said they would take a hunter using a .30-06 with an appropriate load, provided the hunter is very familiar and proficient with his rifle and load. Otherwise, he wants his hunters to use a .300 Win. Mag. or larger caliber.

Larry Rivers, master guide from Talkeetna, Alaska, wants his hunters to use at least a .300 Win. Mag. on inland grizzlies and .338 Win. Mag. or .375 H&H Mag. on brown bears. Cy Ford, who guides along the coast of British Columbia, is very specific. He wants his hunters to use a .338 Win. Mag. with a 250-grain Nosler Partition bullet.

The bottom line in caliber selection for a big bear hunt is first to get your guide's recommendation. He is experienced at bear hunting in the area you will be in and will have a definite idea of what you should use. Use a caliber and hunting load that you have practiced with and can hit your target with from 150 yards. I would much rather take a 75-yard shot at a brown bear using a .338 Win. Mag. that I was comfortable shooting and in which I had confidence than to have a powerful .458 Win. Mag. of which I was scared. Poor bullet placement can be the biggest

2,800 Foot-Pounds at 150 Yards

*P*opular rifle calibers and bullet weights that have a retained energy level of 2,800 foot-pounds at 150 yards are:

Cartridge	Bullet Weight (in grains)
.300 Win. Mag.	180
.308 Norma Mag.	180
.300 Wthby Mag.	150 and 180
.300 Rem. Ultra Mag.	180
.30-378 Wthby Mag.	180 and 200
.338 Win. Mag.	200, 225 and 250
.338 Rem. Ultra Mag.	250
.338-378 Wthby Mag.	200, 225 and 250
.340 Wthby Mag.	200 and 250
.375 H&H Mag.	270
.378 Wthby Mag.	300
.416 Rem. Mag.	350 and 400
.416 Rigby	350 and 400
.416 Wthby. Mag.	350 and 400
.458 Win. Mag.	500
.460 Wthby Mag.	500

and deadliest mistake when hunting big bears.

Based on my guide survey, the .30-06 is generally considered too small and the .458 Win. Mag. too large. All cartridges in between these two are considered by most to be much more effective, with the .338 Win. Mag. the top choice, especially if other game, such as caribou or moose, are to be hunted at the same time.

BULLET CONSTRUCTION

Almost all big bear guides want their hunters to use bullets that weigh 200 grains or more and are constructed to hold together for deep penetration and controlled

Get your guide's recommendation for a caliber and load before the hunt. He has seen many bears go down and knows what it takes.

Factory Load Ballistics for Suitable Big Bear Cartridges

Cartridge	Bullet Wt. (grains)	Muzzle Velocity (fps)	Muzzle Energy (fp)	Downrange Energy (fp) 100 Yds.	200 Yds
.30-378 Wthby Mag.	180	3,450	4,757	4,204	3,709
	200	3,160	4,434	3,877	3,381
.300 Rem Ultra Mag.	180	3,250	4,221	3,714	3,260
	200	3,025	4,063	3,547	3,086
.300 Wthby Mag.	180	3,300	4,300	3,753	3,226
	220	2,905	4,000	3,050	2,206
.300 H&H Mag.	180	2,880	3,315	2,785	2,325
.300 Win. Mag.	180	2,960	3,503	3,012	2,579
	220	2,680	3,510	2,928	2,426
.308 Norma Mag.	180	3,020	3,646	3,168	2,740
8mm Rem. Mag.	185	3,080	3,898	3,132	2,495
	220	2,830	3,913	3,255	2,689
.338-.378 Wthby Mag.	200	3,350	4,983	4,391	3,861
	225	3,180	5,052	4,420	3,856
	250	3,060	5,197	4,528	3,933
.338 Win. Mag.	200	2,960	3,892	3,138	2,506
	225	2,780	3,862	3,306	2,816
.338 Rem. Ultra Mag.	250	2,830	4,540	3,882	3,303
.340 Wthby Mag.	200	3,210	4,577	3,857	3,228
	210	3,180	4,717	3,996	3,365
	250	2,850	4,510	3,515	2,710
.375 H&H Mag.	270	2,690	4,339	3,512	2,813
	300	2,530	4,265	3,427	2,724
.378 Wthby Mag.	270	3,180	6,064	4,688	3,570
	300	2,925	5,700	4,380	3,325
.416 Wthby Mag.	350	2,850	6,312	5,553	4,870
	400	2,700	6,474	5,189	4,113
.416 Rigby	400	2,370	5,115	4,050	3,165
	410	2,370	4,990	4,110	3,350
.416 Rem. Mag.	400	2,400	5,115	4,201	3,419
.458 Win. Mag.	510	2,040	4,714	3,549	2,641
.460 Wthby Mag.	500	2,700	8,095	6,370	4,968

expansion.

For the kinetic energy to be transferred from the bullet entering the animal's body into the shock waves which destroy the animal's nervous system, the bullet must be constructed to expand in a controlled fashion as it travels into the animal. It is this mushrooming, or bulldozer effect, of the expanding bullet that transfers the energy and causes the deadly hydrostatic shock.

Key: Controlled Expansion & Penetration

A thin-jacketed bullet will break up on impact with a grizzly's shoulder, while a steel-jacketed bullet may pass completely through the bear's body, transferring little energy, causing little hydrostatic shock and thus not putting the animal down. Instead, controlled expansion and penetration, with retention of much of the original weight, are the necessary features for a big bear bullet.

In order to achieve this, the bullet must be constructed so that the core will stay in the jacket to guarantee the retained weight necessary for adequate penetration. This is done by locking the core to the jacket. A Bitterroot bullet, the choice of many bear hunters, gives this desired result by having a heavy copper-tubing jacket bonded to the lead core so that jacket and core will not separate.

The Nosler Partition, perhaps the most popular bullet in use by bear hunters today, locks the core to

Nosler partition bullet—an excellent choice for dealing with shots at big bears.

the jacket to ensure mass retention by using a partition in the jacket. The forward core expands, while the rear core stays intact.

The selection of high-quality factory loads in the big-bear calibers is constantly growing. Ammunition manufacturers such as Remington, Winchester, Federal, Norma, Weatherby and Hornady offer enough choices that the most discriminating hunter can find a factory load that will shoot well in his rifle.

HANDLOADS

Many hunters now handload ammunition, and by testing a wide variety of loads in their rifles, they can usually obtain better results than with factory loads. However, guides offer a word of caution in regard to handloading ammunition for bear hunting. More misfires occur on hunts when handloads are used.

The handloading hunter should consider that one primer with a small amount of case lube on it may cost him the trophy of a lifetime. Or, the guide may have to finish off a bear in case a second or third shot is necessary and the hunter's rifle won't fire. I have personally seen the look on a hunter's face when his handloads wouldn't fire at a trophy grizzly slowly walking across a clearing 75 yards away. It can make the trip off a mountain long and silent ... or worse. Think about it.

Big Bears, Big Guns

RIFLES FOR BIG BEARS

*R*ifle selection is a personal matter, with most hunters having some very definite opinions on which is the best rifle for a particular species of big game. The same is true with bear rifles, except some thought must be given to the fact that a bear can be a dangerous critter, and a second, third and fourth shot may be necessary to get the job done properly.

Some bear hunters want the firepower of a semiautomatic rifle, while others want the challenge and accuracy of a single-shot rifle. A few even choose the double rifle.

Most hunters and virtually every bear guide with whom I have discussed rifles prefer a good bolt-action rifle. Bolt-actions are quick and simple to use, accurate, and can take the abusive weather and other conditions that come with hunting big bears. Reliability is more than important. And while they don't have the rapid firepower of the semiautomatic, they do offer a third or fourth shot, and in some cases, a fifth, should such be required.

RIFLE NOTES

When you are preparing for your hunt, keep in mind that some rifles come from the factory with poor accuracy built in, and most will shoot one load more accurately than others. In fact, your rifle may not shoot some loads accurately enough for hunting dangerous game.

There is only one way to check out a bear rifle's accuracy: Spend several days on the range shooting the rifle

Miscellaneous Rifle Accessories

Since bear hunting can mean hours of walking, often up steep slopes, across swollen creeks, on snow slides and many times on snowshoes, a sling is an important addition to a rifle. Every bear hunter should also know how to shoot using a sling position, both sitting and kneeling. Bear hunting is not the place for unaided, off-hand shooting. A sling can give you the edge if no other rest is available.

Also be sure to carry a compact rifle cleaning kit with you. A rifle takes a lot of abuse on a bear hunt, and a nightly cleaning is a good idea; in wet weather, it's a *must*.

Another shooting accessory the bear hunter should have is a strong, lockable, hard-bodied gun case to pack your rifle in while flying commercially. From that point on, you will want a well-padded soft case to protect your rifle when in bush planes or in boats.

Finally, if you are going on a horseback hunt, check with your guide in advance to see if he furnishes a saddle scabbard or if you need to. If it's up to you, consider a Cordura scabbard; hard-sided scabbards do the job well, too. I have found both of them to do a better job of protecting my rifle than traditional leather scabbards.

from a benchrest with a variety of bear hunting loads until you are satisfied that you have an accurate rifle matched to a good hunting load. For my own bear hunting, I want a heavy caliber rifle that is capable of shooting a two-inch, five-shot group at 150 yards with my hunting load.

Scopes & Mounting Them

At the time you are doing this range work, you should be shooting with the same scope on your rifle that you intend to use on your bear hunt. Rifle scopes and mounting systems take a pounding on these big rifles shooting powerful loads, and occasionally they will shoot loose or a reticle will move. Get the best rifle scope and mounting system you can find, and watch it carefully as you do your range work.

The selection of a rifle scope for bear hunting is easy if that is the only species of game to be hunted. Most guides agree that the best range is within 100 yards to give the shooter the best target possible for proper bullet placement and to have as much energy as possible remaining in the bullet. Most guides don't want a shot over 150 yards, and shots over 100 yards are usually reserved only for proven marksmen at a good target. For safety reasons, some guides avoid stalks that put the hunter at ranges less than

50 yards. Not many bears go down in their tracks with one shot.

Low power is best. Considering the short ranges within which bears are likely to be shot, most hunters prefer a 1X or 1.5X scope for hunting brown bears in the thick cover found along the coast. If longer shots are anticipated, a 1.5X to 5X is great. It can be turned down in thick cover and moved up for bears feeding on open slides or tidal flats. If other game, such as moose or caribou, is to be hunted with the rifle, a higher-powered variable scope may be chosen. However, the variable should include a power at least as low as 2X for the really close shots.

Buy the best. As with all your equipment, your choice of rifle scope should be the best you can afford. Wet conditions, heavy recoil, bumps and knocks day after day in boats or on stalks will take a heavy toll on cheap scopes. It is sad to see a once-in-a-lifetime hunt ruined by a fogged scope or one that won't hold a zero. This is not the place to cut corners to pay the plane fare.

Big Bears, Big Guns

Chapter Six

HANDGUNS, BOWS & MUZZLELOADERS

or some inexplicable reason, pounding him with a high-powered, magnum-class rifle wasn't enough for you. You took the one-shot challenge, and here you are with a muzzleloader or bow in hand, or maybe a handgun, aiming at a bear that could kill you with one swipe of a paw and eat you for hors d'oeuvres. He stands twenty or maybe fifty yards away: close, too close for comfort. If you decide to go one of these routes with your weaponry—the challenge is great—you need to think about a lot of factors, and plan carefully. Here's how.

THE ONE SHOT CHALLENGE

Hunting big bears with a modern rifle is a challenge, as there is some risk involved. Even with multiple shot capability, the first shot is what it's all about.

But some hunters want an even greater challenge and choose to hunt big bears with either a handgun, bow or muzzleloading rifle. Any of these three means of taking a bear requires that the hunter get as close to his game as possible. That's the challenge. That's the danger. That's the excitement!

Most of the handguns suitable for taking big bears are single-shot, meaning a good first shot to break down the bear is a must, as the second shot is slow in coming.

Bowhunters know that an arrow kills a bear by causing hemorrhaging and that the bear will stay on his feet for at least a few critical seconds—plenty of time for a charge, even after taking a hit in the vitals.

The muzzleloading rifle hunter usually has single-shot capacity, unless a double rifle is used. And, due to the cloud of white smoke it produces when fired, the muzzleloading rifle identifies the position of the

shooter for the bear instantly.

In short, any one of these three methods of bear hunting can be one of the greatest—and scariest—challenges in the hunting world!

ARE YOU READY?

Who should attempt a challenge of this magnitude?

Obviously, the first answer to this question is: one who has mastered the skill of shooting the handgun, bow or muzzleloading rifle. Each of the three requires hours upon hours of practice to master the marksmanship necessary to make the first shot count ... even when hands are wet and cold, knees are shaking from excitement and the body is heaving from an exhausting stalk.

Next, the hunter must have the ability to pin-point the exact spot on the bear he wants to hit. A big bear at 15 yards is a massive target, but little of that mass is the target you want to hit. It requires some study and a lot of concentration and self-

Let the Guide Know

*H*ere's some common-sense advice. Be sure to discuss your weapon and hunting method with your guide from the very beginning. After you have booked your hunt is the wrong time to spring the news on your guide that you plan to use a handgun, bow or muzzleloading rifle. The fact is that some guides don't want to take hunters who hunt with these devices. Some will take you, others won't. Keep in mind that with the handgun, bow or muzzleloader, a lot of respon-sibility falls upon you to be skillful with its use ... and on your guide to be ready to possibly save your hide if things don't go well.

None of the guides I know want to go into the devil's club and alder thickets after a wounded bear, so don't be surprised if they make you prove you can shoot your handgun, bow or muzzleloader as well as you say you can. Be up-front about all your hunting plans when talking to your guide, and both of you will be glad in the end.

control when the moment of truth arrives.

The third part of the answer to this question was given to me by my friend Bob Good, a nationally-known handgun hunter who has taken brown bears with a single-shot handgun. Good acknowledges that grizzlies and brown bears have been successfully taken by handgun hunters, and will continue to be, but cautions that a hunt for either of these should be conducted with extreme caution and care.

"The hunter should always be backed up by an experienced, competent guide armed with a heavy caliber rifle," Good advises. "The guide should understand that getting a bear with a handgun is important to you, and that once he fires and hits the bear, it cannot be classified as a handgun kill (for trophy records). He must be experienced enough on bears to rapidly judge if your hits are going to be quickly fatal to the bear, or if you may be put in a life-threatening situation. And you must have trust and confidence in your backup, so that if he fires, you don't come all unglued because he felt he had to fire to protect your collective posteriors from a potential chewing. Remember that the personal safety of the guide and hunter must be paramount at all times. If there is the slightest question, the guide should shoot instantly, and since it will always be a judg-ment call, you must be willing to abide by the call. If you are not willing to accept those conditions, then don't hunt the big bear, or any other dangerous game for that matter."

This advice applies equally to bowhunters and muzzleloading rifle hunters. Since there are relatively few of us who can legally hunt big bears without a guide, having a qualified backup is usually automatic. What you need to be sure of is that the guide understands the special requirements and constraints of hunting with a handgun, bow or muzzleloader.

Practice until you're 100 percent confident that your first shot will meet its exact target before you go bear hunting with a muzzleloader.

99   Handguns, Bows & Muzzleloaders

HANDGUNNING FOR BEARS

THE MYTH OF THE .44 MAG

Mention hunting big bears with a handgun, and someone will quickly start talking about the .44 Mag. and all its power. The fact of the matter is that the .44 Mag. is not the most powerful handgun caliber in the world, as movies and TV would have us believe, and it is not a good choice for big bears. Granted, some big bears have been taken with a .44 Mag., but even most of those hunters will admit that the caliber is marginal on a bear that is totally calm when shot ... and even less effective on an excited bear.

Handgun Where-To

If you want to hunt big bears with a handgun, go to Alaska. Nonresidents cannot take a handgun into Canada, and handgun ownership of residents is very limited. If you are a Canadian resident, check with your local laws to see if you can hunt big bears with a handgun there.

I heard about a hunter who was going to the Yukon for a spring grizzly hunt. At the last moment, he decided to leave his rifle at home, and he took his hunting handgun. His hunt was abruptly stopped at the border. So if you want to hunt with your handgun, think Alaska.

Handgunning Accessories

*S*ince the Thompson/Center Contender is a single-shot pistol, anyone considering hunting dangerous game such as bears should wear a wrist-band cartridge holder to make reloading faster. It holds six cartridges in a fast and easy-to-get-to position. Also available: a sturdy nylon shoulder holster for the scoped T/C Contender, which is a convenient way to carry the handgun when hunting in grizzly country. It leaves the hands free for moving limbs or climbing. Check your shooting catalogs.

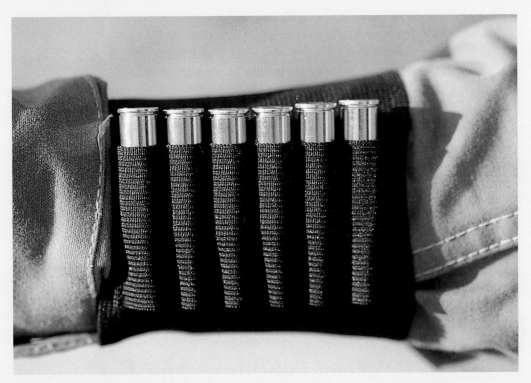

Single-shot handgun hunters should use a wristband to hold ammo for quick second shots.

.454 Casull

The revolver that is probably getting the most attention from big bear handgun hunters is the .454 Casull. It comes in barrel lengths from $4^3/4$ to $7^1/2$ inches, with most big bear hunters choosing the longer. These are extremely strong five-shot, single-action revolvers chambered in .454 Casull that can generate more than a ton of energy at the muzzle, nearly twice that of a .44 Mag. In fact, the .454 Casull 300-grain factory load delivers more energy at 200 yards than the .44 Mag., 240-grain factory load

has at the muzzle.

I think we will see a number of record book grizzlies and brown bears being taken with this pistol, as it is has found favor with a growing number of hunters. If a bear hunter feels compelled to carry a backup sidearm, I would heartily recommend the .454 Casull over the .44 Mag.

.375 JDJ

The most popular caliber for big bears among handgun hunters is the .375 JDJ, and with good rea-

Handgun Scopes

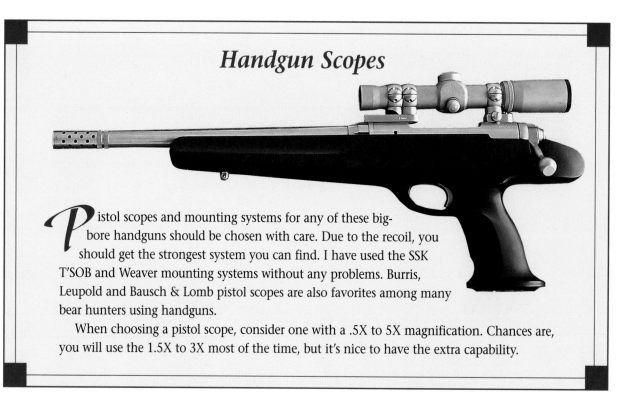

Pistol scopes and mounting systems for any of these big-bore handguns should be chosen with care. Due to the recoil, you should get the strongest system you can find. I have used the SSK T'SOB and Weaver mounting systems without any problems. Burris, Leupold and Bausch & Lomb pistol scopes are also favorites among many bear hunters using handguns.

When choosing a pistol scope, consider one with a .5X to 5X magnification. Chances are, you will use the 1.5X to 3X most of the time, but it's nice to have the extra capability.

son. Numerous big bears shot with this caliber have gone down without any trouble. The .375 JDJ is a wildcat caliber developed by firearms expert J.D. Jones. It is a .444 Marlin case necked down to accept the .375 bullet. It has prairie-dog accuracy out to distances much farther than anyone should be shooting at a bear and enough energy to kill an elephant.

The firearm that shoots this outstanding cartridge is a Thompson/Center Contender outfitted with an SSK Industries .375 JDJ Barrel.

I consider the .375 JDJ caliber in the T/C Contender to be one of the all-time best big bear

Factory Load Ballistics for Big Bear Handgun Calibers

Caliber	Bullet Wt. (Grs.)	Muzzle Velocity (fps)	Muzzle Energy (fp)	Downrange Energy (fp) 50 Yds.	100 Yds.
.44 Rem. Mag.	240	1,180	741	623	543
.454 Casull	240	1,875	1,873	1,494	1,186
	260	1,800	1,870	1,516	1,225
	300	1,600	1,705	1,417	1,181
.375 JDJ	270	1,990	2,373	2,198	2,043
.45-70	400	1,631	2,365	2,150	1,995

The .454 Casull, .375 JDJ and .45-70 all make good big bear cartridges for handgunners. The .44 Rem. Mag. doesn't quite cut the mustard.

handgun hunting combinations. When used with a quality mounting system and a good pistol scope, 1.5-inch groups at 100 yards can be expected from hunting loads.

.45-70

Another good caliber for handgun hunting big bear is the .45-70, which is also available in several versions to shoot from the T/C Contender or T/C Encore systems. There are also some oversized revolver models available chambered in .45-70.

It is accurate, and as J.D. Jones puts it, "... the best 150-yard sledgehammer for hunting available in the Contender," which puts it well within grizzly range. Some excellent factory loaded ammunition is available for this caliber, and handloads with the Speer 400-grain bullet do a good job, expanding to about .85 inch. Cast bullets also work well in .45-70 loads.

When using a single-shot handgun, you must place your first shot well. Contrary to popular belief, when the proper caliber/load is used by a competent shooter, large bears can be taken with handguns.

BOWHUNTING FOR BEARS

I had the good fortune of hunting with the late Fred Bear for several hunting seasons, and it was always the highlight of the hunt to hear Fred tell about his big bear hunts. During his long hunting career, he took polar, brown and grizzly bears with a bow.

A Fred Bear Story

The last time Fred and I hunted together, he told me that his greatest hunt ever was a brown bear hunt he took during the early 1960s. Fred, his guide and a photographer were checking out a beach area

from a small boat. When they rounded a small point, they saw a big brown walking out of the alders onto the beach about a half-mile away. The hunters shut off the boat motor and slowly, quietly made their way to the beach while the bear proceeded to feed on something in the sand. At one point, the bear waded into the water and lay on his back with only his head and feet sticking out.

The hunters crept onto the beach, unnoticed by the bear, and got out of the boat for the stalk. Fred had his 65-pound Kodiak recurve bow with four arrows tipped with Bear Razorheads. The guide and the photographer were armed with rifles in case backup was needed.

As they started the stalk, they were surprised to see the bear coming toward them. The photographer set up right where he was on the beach. Fred and the guide made their way closer to the bear to the only cover on the beach, a large rock. The bear continued to close the distance, ambling along at the water's edge. They waited.

Finally the bear came by at 25 feet, between the hunters and the water, where he paused to look over the rock and two objects. Satisfied, he turned broadside to walk on.

Fred drew and released the arrow. It sank to the feathers behind the front leg. The bear bellowed and headed down the beach straight for the photographer. The photographer stood his ground, taking pictures until the bear filled the frame of his camera, then he ran for cover. The mortally wounded bear ran by him at full speed.

Near the boat, the bear tried to get into an alder thicket, but died and rolled down to the water's edge.

The arrow had hit a rib near the front leg, passed through a lung, cut an artery near the liver, then went through the diaphragm and through the skin near the ribs on the opposite side. He died in less than a minute, but covered 90 yards during his last seconds. The bear was weighed on scales by using the winch on the large boat Fred and his group were using as a base camp. It weighed 810 pounds. The hide squared nine feet, and the skull measured 27 inches.

This story is proof that there is a place in big bear hunting for the properly prepared bowhunter.

THE ULTIMATE CHALLENGE

Some, especially those who've done it, would argue that bowhunting one of the big-three bears is the ultimate hunting adventure and challenge to be had on the North American continent. The reason is simple: it pits the fiercest animals against the most primitive hunting tool. To most bowhunters, this is the pinnacle—the hunt they bowhunt their entire lives to prepare for.

This should not be a hunt you plan early in your bowhunting career. Only when you've been seasoned by deer, elk, moose and black bears, and have faced all of them under a wide variety of conditions, should you consider yourself ready for a toe-to-toe test with a big bear.

At that point, you will have settled on the bowhunting gear that works best for you. A lot of big bears have been killed by archers using traditional gear like longbows and recurves. And, in skilled hands, those bows are still efficient hunting tools. But most bowhunters maximize their potential by using a compound bow. Hundreds of compound models and variations are available. Which make or model you buy is not as important as your ability to shoot it well.

Shooting your bow well must be taken to the Nth degree. In all likelihood, you'll be on the ground facing a moving, menacing animal. The shot, if it comes at all, will likely only be there for a matter of a couple seconds. If you cannot quickly calculate the range, draw your bow and put your arrow in an apple-sized spot, you're not ready.

Chuck Adams's preference for a finger release offers some advantages in this type of a bowhunt. You will be more shaken than you've ever been. You cannot afford to fumble while attaching your mechanical release aid to the bowstring. Remember, you might have a second or two. Shooting your bow

Calculating Kinetic Energy

Here is the formula for calculating the kinetic energy (KE) of your setup. You need a minimum KE of 60 pounds to hunt big bears like grizzly, brown and polar bears.

$$KE = \frac{\text{arrow weight in grains} \times \text{velocity}^2}{450{,}240}$$

For example, a bow shooting an arrow shaft weighing 525 grains and leaving the bow at 250 feet per second (fps) has a kinetic energy of 72.88 foot-pounds of energy.

well means not just being able to hit the target; it means getting your bow drawn and releasing efficiently.

Of course, the bow and arrow combination that you choose must also generate sufficient kinetic energy (KE) to do the job on these huge animals. According to *North American Hunter* "Bowhunting" columnist Chuck Adams, who's taken all of North America's bears with a bow, 60 foot-pounds is the minimum energy requirement for your setup.

The KE calculation is simple to do with a calculator as long as you know your arrow weight and speed. Take the arrow speed, or velocity, (in feet per second) squared, times the arrow weight (in grains, broadhead included), and divide by 450,240. The formula is shown above. That will give you kinetic energy right out of the bow.

To calculate it further, you'll have to reference a computer program from Easton aluminum that simulates downrange performance, or use a chronograph to calculate your downrange arrow speed. Kinetic energy is the key to arrow penetration. Arrow placement and penetration are the keys to taking game cleanly. And if there's any big game animal that requires you to know every detail about your setup, it's a big polar bear, brown or griz.

The same focus must be applied to your arrow/broadhead combination. Here Adams opts for a finished arrow that weighs at least 500 grains.

Heavier arrows are better at absorbing a bow's energy and retaining that energy downrange. As for the broadhead, it must be shaving-sharp and super-tough. An expandable broadhead is virtually out of the question because of the reduced penetration and the risks you and your guide assume if the mechanical head fails to function properly.

For big bears, choose a fixed-blade design with a wide cutting diameter. With the help of your archery shop professional, narrow the field to a few options that meet the above requirements and then select the model that tunes best with your bow and arrow setup. For what it's worth, Adams chose a Zwickey Black Diamond head to take his polar bear (1,000 pounds), brown bear (1,300 pounds) and grizzly (600 pounds), and cleanly took those bears with a bow generating approximately 62 foot-pounds of energy.

The distance at which you can group those broadhead-tipped arrows inside a 4-inch diameter circle is your maximum effective range for big bears. An 8-inch circle is often the guideline given for deer hunting proficiency with a bow, but deer don't bite and they don't have sharp claws.

ONLY ONE CHANCE

Putting the danger aside, just how important your one shot can be may be reflected in the success or failure of an expensive hunt. When polar bear hunting was still permitted in Alaska, the legendary Fred Bear hunted the great white polar bear off the coast of Barrow on the pack ice.

The hunt started April 13, and it was May 11 before a bear was sighted. Fred, the guide, and another hunter got in front of the bear's expected route and waited to ambush the slow-moving bear. They waited for $1^{1}/_{2}$ hours in a pile of ice before they spotted the bear ambling their way. At a distance of a quarter mile, the bear changed his direction of travel. The hunters cautiously changed their location to cut the bear off. Now the bear was coming toward them, but it stopped at 50 yards out, sniffing and looking toward the hunters' ice cover. Fred decided this was going to be his only shot. He rose and shot. The arrow hit the bear behind the shoulder, and he went down, biting at the arrow in his side. Then, rising again, the bear started running over a pressure ridge; however, he had covered only 100 yards before he

The success or failure of a bowhunter hunting big bear rests in that all-important first shot.

again, the bear started running over a pressure ridge; however, he had covered only 100 yards before he fell dead.

This one shot was all Fred got after 25 days of bad weather. It pays to have your act together if you plan to hunt big bears with a bow.

Handguns, Bows & Muzzleloaders

MUZZLELOADING FOR BEARS

Muzzleloading rifle hunters have several problems unique to their sport that can make bear hunting dangerous. The first problem is that muzzleloading rifles can be downright cranky about firing in the wet conditions in which a lot of bear hunting takes place.

Next, when a bear is within 50 or so yards and the muzzleloading rifle hunter fires, he had better break the bear down. The noise, the cloud of white smoke and the sulfur smell of the burning powder help the bear pinpoint the hunter's location.

Also, most muzzleloading rifles are one-shot firearms, with the reloading process taking about a minute. In the meantime, if the bear decides to charge, there is little that can be done but for you to let the guide finish the job you started.

Muzzleloading rifles that are best suited for large

bear are .50 caliber or larger. It should fire its projectile with a muzzle velocity of at least 1,700 feet per second (fps) to get enough downrange energy to break a bear down in the shoulder.

BULLETS

The projectile you elect to use in the muzzleloading rifle should be selected with care. While there is no modern experience at hand to help guide the hunter into selecting the right ball or bullet, there is plenty of documentation from early explorers who encountered grizzlies regularly to know that round balls made of soft lead were not the best choice for putting the big bear down. In most cases, these hunters depended upon several guns firing several times into a bear. Based on my studies of history and knowing something about what a bear can take and yet stay on his feet, I would rule out round balls.

Some of the conical lead bullets available give excellent results on game such as elk, caribou and moose and would probably be sufficient on a grizzly in the hands of a skilled hunter. Today's modern, saboted rifle and pistol bullets are probably the best choice.

A number of muzzleloading rifles are on today's market in the .50 and .54 caliber range that might be considered for big bear hunting. While there may be allure in hunting with a traditional style rifle, the best and most efficient choice is one of the modern, in-line guns which are the most reliable and tend to be the most accurate with saboted bullets.

Since this is a game animal which usually requires more than one shot, double rifles, such as Connecticut Valley Arms' .50 caliber percussion Express Rifle or .50 caliber percussion Over/Under Rifle, might be a good choice.

I definitely suggest a rifle with a percussion ignition system over a flintlock system due to the wet conditions usually associated with bear hunting in the Far North.

Muzzleloading Accessories

Accessories that would be important to the muzzleloading rifle shooter hunting dangerous bears include a capper with plenty of caps in it tied around your neck so you could get to it in a hurry, and a coat pocket with several speed-load tubes in it. You can premeasure an amount of powder in one end of the tube and place a lubricated conical bullet in the other. This can speed up the reloading process greatly.

If I were going after a grizzly right now with a muzzleloading rifle, I would want a high-quality, percussion system .54 caliber double rifle with 1:17 twist barrels. On it I would choose a conical bullet that would give maximum controlled penetration. I would work on loads until I found one that would give me a muzzle velocity of at least an 1,800 fps . Then I would employ a guide who was good with a .338 Win. Mag.

Chapter Seven

SHOT PLACEMENT

*P*age through this chapter quickly. How many pages are here, talking about shot placement? Yes, that's right—16 pages. That should give you an idea of how vitally important proper shot placement is on a big bear. One picture and a few words won't do it: You have to understand how tough big bears are, how essential it is that you put your bullet or arrow exactly where it needs to go so it can do its job effectively ... and how to go after a wounded bear without losing your pants (or worse, your life) when you have to go in after him. Bottom line? Place your first shot precisely and correctly. Here's how.

Tough &
Tenacious Customers

*P*roper shot placement is important on all game, but it is more important on big bears than on any other critter hunted in North America simply because a poorly-shot bear can bite back. I saw this demonstrated early in my hunting career many years ago while on a fall caribou hunt.

Runaway Hunter

One of our hunters had a grizzly license he hoped to fill out. Early one morning, he and I were sitting on a steep tundra hill, glassing the vast valley below for caribou. I saw movement near the bottom of the same hill we were on, and when I put my glasses on it, I saw a grizzly plowing up a rockpile, digging for ground squirrels. The wind was blowing from the grizzly to us, so we began closing the distance to the busy bear.

The hunter with me had already demonstrated his shooting ability with his custom .300 Wthby Mag. back at the base camp. He could shoot a five-shot group at 100 yards that printed almost like one hole. We had talked at length, looking at a picture of a bear, about where he should hold on a grizzly to break the shoulders should we come upon one. We had also agreed that if he got an opportunity at a grizzly, he wouldn't stop shooting until the bear stopped moving.

Confident in the hunter's ability, I motioned for him to follow, and we went from alder patch to alder patch to get within shooting range of the bear. Near the end of our stalk, we ran out of cover and had to crawl to a depression that looked like a terrace in the side of the hill. When we got there, we were well-hidden and in a perfect position to look down the hill some 140 yards to where the unsuspecting bear was still trying to figure out how to catch a squirrel.

The hunter took off his jacket and rolled it up to rest his rifle on for a steady shot. I lay my rifle down and got on my belly to watch the bear through binoculars. The bear was broadside to us, giving the hunter a perfect shot.

It seemed like an hour went by before the Weatherby roared in my right ear. I heard the bullet strike the bear, but it sounded like it hit a drum. Howling, the bear spun around, biting himself in the side. Around and around he spun, still howling. The grizzly was obviously gutshot.

I waited for the second shot, but none came. Suddenly the bear stopped spinning, and with eyes fixed on me—eyes that looked afire—he started running up the steep slope, foam flowing from his mouth.

Time was critical now. I grabbed my rifle and shot. The bear took the hit in his chest and rolled to one side, but by the time I bolted in another round, he was getting up. I fired again, this time hitting his lower jaw with tremendous damage. He bawled and shook his head, slinging blood everywhere, and started moving in my direction again. This time I picked out his right shoulder and put a bullet in it. He fell and started rolling down the hill.

I bolted in my last round, hoping I wouldn't have to use it. But the bear caught the tundra in his claws, stopped rolling and, looking at me through a bloody face,

The gut shot bear headed straight for me, and my client stopped shooting. I had little time to stop the charge.

pulled himself up again. This time, I put my final round under his now-destroyed chin. He sank to the ground, finished.

Now that the crisis was over, I realized two things: First, the bear was just a few yards in front of me, and second, my hunting companion—who never fired a second shot—was not beside me. Shaking and weak, I turned and saw him scrambling up the slope behind me as fast as he could go. It all made sense now. The bear probably never saw me. When the hunter realized he had made a bad first shot, he jumped up and started running up the slope. Then the gutshot bear saw the cause of all his misery and started running after it with revenge in his heart. I just happened to be in the middle.

This misadventure taught me a lesson that I will never forget about shot placement on a bear.

A WILL TO LIVE

To understand why a big bear is so hard to put down for keeps, one must know something about

Shot Placement

Being at the top of the food chain means that he has little to fear.

the bear. First of all, the bear is at the top of the food chain and has been for centuries; therefore, it has no inherent fear of any living creature. When the first explorers came upon grizzlies, they were shocked at the animals' lack of fear. Grizzly, brown and polar bears still demonstrate this bold behavior.

Add to this lack of fear a degree of tenacity not seen in any other animal. Big bears have a will to live that is unequaled by any other creature and will fight to their last breath to survive. Wounds and injuries that would kill lesser animals often do not slow down big bears.

Survivors

Stories abound in the Far North about bears being shot, often repeatedly, only to be seen again the next year. One such bear made a name for himself in the panhandle of Alaska in the 1950s. This bear terrorized a river system with its loud roaring, enough to keep fishermen away from the river for years.

When hunters finally killed the bear, the reason for its belligerence was found: a rifle bullet embedded in its skull next to the brain. The bullet, which had been shot into the bear years before, had fractured the skull, and the skull grew back into a grotesque shape. Such an injury would have killed most animals.

Another example of how much punishment a bear can take and go on living was related to me by Alaska guide Bob Hannon. One of his bear hunting camps is near the village of Koyuk. A native fish camp in the area had been terrorized by a big bear for six years. Late each August, when the local fishermen were drying their fish on outdoor fish racks for the coming winter, the big bear would come into the camp and destroy two months' work in one night. This cut drastically into the families' winter food supply. The bear, which they called "The Rogue," knew no fear and would come into the camp to get the fish no matter what the consequences. He had been shot many times.

The local people asked Hannon to kill the bear for them, as they had suffered enough grief at the hands of this calculating raider. So Hannon moved his camp there and put one of his hunters on the bear, bringing its reign of terror to an almost anticlimactic end. On the second day of the hunt, the bear was quickly killed at 45 yards with a .338 Win. Mag. Browning semi-automatic BAR. The bear's hide squared 9 feet 3 inches, and the skull scored over 25 points.

But it wasn't until Hannon skinned the bear that he was sure they had taken "The Rogue." In skinning the bear, he found that the left front leg had a .22 bullet embedded in the wrist bone. The hams had been shot through with a high-powered rifle at one time, but the massive wound had healed up nicely. The entire face was carrying a load of No. 6 shot, and at some point, the bear had been shot in the face with 00 buckshot, as one of the pellets was lodged in the jaw where it had been broken and healed over. This wound alone meant that the bear probably didn't eat anything for about six weeks while the jaw was healing, a testament to just how tenacious a bear can be.

THEY DON'T DIE EASILY

In addition to his lack of fear and will to live, a big bear has an awesome physical structure to contend with. He is built to withstand tremendous shock. An old Indian that I used to hunt with would say, "The griz is a ball of muscle and solid bone wrapped up in a tough skin."

There's a lot of truth in that, and you really believe it when you skin and butcher a grizzly, brown or polar bear. Its bones, especially the small ones, are almost solid. They house little marrow. A meat saw has a tough time sawing through them. Layer upon layer of massive muscles are tightly laced to this tough frame. Protecting that is a layer of fat. The outer layer is tough skin and thick hair. The shooter must shoot through all of that before he hits the vitals.

If the bear sees you, catches your scent, hears you or if anything else excites him at the moment you shoot, a charge of adrenaline is sent through his body that can keep him on his feet and moving unless hit in his spine or brain, or unless his shoulders are badly broken.

A wounded, super-charged bear that is still on his feet can pose a couple of perilous problems as long as life remains in his body. One, if he has a fix on you, he may charge. Two, if thick cover is nearby, he may run into the cover. This can be as frightening as having him run toward you, because now you have to go into thick brush after a wounded grizzly that may well be alive, angry and ready to pounce on you. This is a very important point to remember when hunting in country where cover is only a leap away from the bear.

The ideal situation is to shoot a totally unsuspecting bear that is calmly going about his business. It is this type of bear that hunters, especially

Built like a tank, a bear can withstand unbelievable shock and stay on his feet.

bowhunters, take with one well-placed shot.

Hard to Put Down for Keeps

An example of what an excited grizzly can do and how hard he can be to put down was related to me by handgun hunter Larry Kelly, president of Mag-na-port International, Inc. While camping in a small shack on a river in Alaska, Kelly and his guide were watching a grizzly feed along the river. When the bear saw the two hunters watching him, he started up the riverbank at a fast pace in their direction. The guide fired two warning shots near the bear.

At the second shot, two things happened: The guide's rifle jammed, and the bear came in at a full run. The two hunters ran into the shack with the adrenaline-charged bear hot on their heels. As the bear came through the door, Kelly fired his Smith & Wesson Model 29 .44 Mag. revolver into the bear's chest at two feet. The bear spun around. Then the guide, with his rifle back in operation, began firing. When the bear finally gave up, the men had put 14 shots into its body. Kelly, who has killed big grizzlies with a handgun using only one shot, knows first-hand the difference between an excited bear with a normal flow of adrenaline and an excited bear that is super-charged by adrenaline.

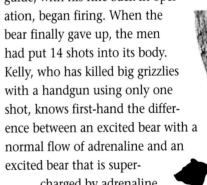
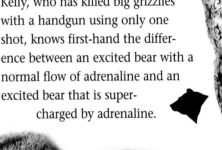

PICKING YOUR SHOT

ou've now heard many stories of how tough it is to kill a big bear. That brings up this important question, one on which your life may depend: Where should you hit a big bear to put it down as quickly, safely and humanely as possible?

SHOULDER SHOT!

Virtually every bear guide and experienced hunter I surveyed or have ever hunted with agrees that with a centerfire rifle, the first shot should strike the bear in the shoulder to break it and anchor the animal. This prevents a charge at the hunter and keeps the animal from reaching brush.

The recommendation for subsequent shots varies among guides, but most prefer the second, third and fourth shot, if necessary, to be in the shoulder-lung area. A few guides like the second shot in the neck, provided the hunter is close to the animal and is a good marksman; this may be an "iffy" proposition because the target is so small.

TAKING THE SHOULDER SHOT

Most experienced bear guides I surveyed have a policy of continuing to shoot a bear in the vital area around the shoulder until it is down for keeps. A common policy is that the hunter make the first shot in the shoulder to put the bear down, and then keep shooting into the shoulder-lung area. Many of these guides have never had a close call with a bear one of their hunters shot, and trailing wounded bears is kept to a minimum. A good taxidermist can patch up the holes.

A bear quartering away gives the hunter the opportunity to take out the lungs and the opposite-side shoulder.

Shot Placement—Shoulder Shot

The shoulder shot is relatively easy to take if the bear is standing broadside and the hunter has the presence of mind to take his time and pick his shot. An ideal hold is with the cross of the scope reticle on the center of the shoulder, with the vertical crosshair running up the center of the leg, provided the leg is in the usual all-fours standing position.

When the bear is quartering to or from the hunter, the shoulder shot requires a little more thought. If he is going away, hold in line with the leg on the far side if it is in the normal standing position. If the leg is in the forward stepping position, hold along the front of the leg. If he is quartering to you, hold for the point of the shoulder.

The shoulder target is very small if the bear is facing you. When given a choice, the hunter should wait until the bear offers a broadside shot. Broadside shots are great. Never pass up the opportunity to put a heavy, puncturing bullet through both shoulders if possible. Not only does it anchor the animal, but it often puts bone fragments into the lungs.

If there is no choice and a head-on shot must be taken, the area to hit that will drop the bear is just to the right or left side of the bear's head. Shoot too far to the outside and you will only flesh-wound the bear; shoot too close to the center and you will hit the bear in the face. That's not good for human-bear relations.

Shooting the bear under the chin will put a bullet in the lungs or possibly the heart, which will kill him, but usually not on the spot. If his eyes are fixed on you, the lungs or heart shot probably won't save you from the wrestling match of a lifetime.

A Head-On Shoulder Shot

An example of how a head-on shot can be effective if executed correctly was described to me by Mark Meekin. A sheep hunter he was guiding became very ill, and Meekin left the sheep camp at sundown to seek medical help. As darkness approached, he was making his way down a steep mountain trail as fast as he could when he almost ran head-on with a grizzly. Startled, the bear charged.

Meekin knew his first shot had better be good. He dropped to a kneeling position and held a sight picture on the bear's shoulder just beside the head. Due to the poor light and the bear's movement, the sight picture was difficult at best. The first shot broke the shoulder, spinning the bear around. Meekin emptied

This is the shot all rifle-toting bear hunters want: Take out both shoulders and put the animal on the ground.

117

Shots Not to Take

Contrary to what is sometimes written, or discussed around campfires, the head or neck shot on a big bear is usually not a good idea. Either can be a tough target when a bear is moving. The neck is short, and the only vital area in the neck is the spinal cord, which can be missed easily. If made properly, the head shot destroys the skull. Because bears are scored for trophy classing according to their skulls, this would be a poor place for a hunter to shoot a bear, except in an emergency of course.

An improper head shot can tear away a chunk of the face, leaving you with one mad critter. When shooting at the head, anything short of a bullet in the brain is inadequate. While the head of a bear appears to be a sizable target, I have talked to a lot of old-time bear hunters who tell me about missing the head shot on bears as close as 25 yards. In short, forget the head shot unless there is no other option.

his rifle as fast as he could into the thrashing bear's lung area. When the dust cleared and the bear lay still, it was only 10 yards from where Meekin was kneeling. A miss of the shoulder on that first shot could have been fatal.

A head-on shot is not recommended. Wait for the bear to move into a better position.

FORGET THE HEART SHOT

The so-called heart shot that some hunters talk about is a poor choice for a centerfire rifle shot. The heart sits low in the bear's body and is a small target that's difficult to hit. Heart shots on grizzlies wind up becoming brisket shots, and we're talking about a nonfatal wound that can make the job of searching for the wounded bear in the brush more adventure than you or your guide may want.

Even if the shot is true, a bear can stay on his feet surprisingly long with his heart blown up. He is fatally wounded when the bullet strikes the heart, but he may not drop for a few minutes, allowing him to make his way into an alder thicket or, maybe worse, to you.

The bottom line for gun hunters is to make every effort to make the first shot a well-placed shoulder shot, with follow-up shots in the shoulder-lung area, or in some situations, a neck shot. The hunter and guide should always discuss shot placement and what the hunter is to do after the first shot.

BOW SHOTS

Bowhunters face an entirely different situation. They do not have the capability of breaking down a big bear. Their means of killing is to put a heavy, razor-sharp broadhead deep into the lungs, cutting vital arteries, veins and lung tissue. The archer must be backed by a guide with a rifle in case the bear locates them and decides to go to the source of the trouble. The best shot for the bowhunter is just behind the front leg. To hit the shoulder or gut-shoot the bear can spell disaster.

Most of the bowhunters I have talked to who have taken a big bear with a bow were surprised by how quickly the bear went down after taking the hit. However, I should point out that all these hunters were expert shots and were shooting a bear that was calm and never knew what hit him. The bowhunter should avoid any shot other than the perfect lung shot at an unsuspecting bear within a reasonable range.

Fred Bear, who took as many big bears with a bow as anyone I know, told me that most bears, when hit with an arrow, will turn, howl, bite at the arrow, then run until they drop. In the same breath, however, Fred pointed out what most experienced bear hunters, guides and biologists know: each bear is different and you can't predict what a bear will do.

The bowhunter must be patient and wait for a heart or lung shot.

The Myth of the Upright Bear

A common misconception is that bears are generally seen standing upright. We have all seen movies and illustrations of ferocious grizzlies charging in an upright position. I have even seen a magazine article showing where to shoot the upright, charging grizzly.

The truth of the matter is that bears spend little time walking around on their hind legs like a man. They will stand erect if they are trying to see over vegetation or feeding on or trying to reach something high, but most of the bears you will see or shoot will be on all fours. I have only seen one bear shot standing, and that was a large black bear my wife shot in some dark timber along the British Columbia coast. This bear was not charging, but seemed simply curious about what was in the brush with him.

Chances are, you won't have to make a shot at an upright bear, but if you do, break him down in the shoulders with a rifle or handgun, or put an arrow through his heart and lungs if bowhunting.

Shot Placement

PRACTICING SHOT PLACEMENT

*R*eading about shot placement on an 800- to 1,200-pound bear is one thing, but actually having the self-discipline to pick out a one-square-inch target on the side of a hairy beast half the size of a pickup truck is quite another.

Most guides agree that the mistake that causes most bear hunts to become a blood-trailing adventure is the hunter's inability to hit the "sweet spot." They aim their rifle, handgun or bow at the middle of the critter and let go.

KNOW BEAR ANATOMY

The first thing that the hunter planning a bear hunt should do is study the anatomy of a bear. Memorize the physique of a bear so that you know the location of the bony structure of the shoulders, the lungs and the heart.

Next, you need to look at some life-size bears to study exactly where you would shoot. The best place to do this is at a zoo. Many zoos throughout the country have both grizzly and polar bears that you can watch. If a black bear is all that is available, watch him. Use binoculars to pick out shoulder or lung shots as the bear stands and walks at different angles.

Most guides say that it is much easier to work with hunters who have studied live bears than with a hunter who is seeing his first bear through a riflescope on a tundra slope. Once you begin to feel comfortable at picking out the target area on zoo bears, get some bear targets to use on the range. And practice. Often.

SHOOT OFTEN: PRACTICE!

Several archery supply companies and other target companies sell reasonably-priced bear targets. Take these targets out to your range and practice shooting the same equipment you plan on shooting on your hunt, at the same distances you may be shooting at while hunting. Practice shooting at the right spot. Practice. Often.

Continue your practice in failing light, and shoot from the positions you may have to use on your bear hunt. In the case of rifle shooting, use a tight sling and shoot from a standing, sitting and kneeling posi-

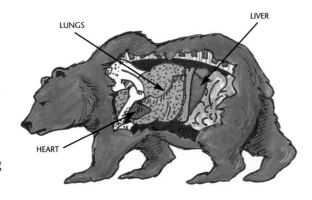

LUNGS LIVER

HEART

All big bear hunters should know bear anatomy so that their shot placement will be right on the money.

tion. Shoot from a rest, such as a post or tree. Concentrate on making first shots that would break the bear's shoulder.

The handgun hunter and bowhunter will want to spend the same amount of time on his shooting positions.

Regardless of what you hunt bears with, bear targets will force you to pick your point, making you proficient at shot placement. You can never practice too much. You're going out after an animal that has no reservations about turning the tables and making you the hunted. Do not take your shooting lightly.

Since most bear hunters will shoot larger calibers than they're used to, a lot of practice is necessary for them to overcome the fear of the rifle and be ready to make that all-important first shot.

DEALING WITH A WOUNDED BEAR

Despite the study of bear anatomy, despite all your practice, a shot may go awry. You and your guide will end up dealing with a wounded bear.

BEST POLICY: DON'T WOUND ONE

All guides agree that the first rule when hunting big bears is not to wound one if gun hunting. If bowhunting, you must stick an arrow in a vital area without the bear ever knowing you are there, then carefully and quietly watch his exit, because you will have to follow him later.

A wounded bear is the most unpredictable animal on earth and can be the most dangerous. Even when they are down, you can't be too cautious.

IS HE DOWN FOR GOOD?

My good friend Charlie Elliot, who for many years thrilled the readers of *Outdoor Life* magazine with his adventures, once told me about a grizzly he shot in Alaska. Wounded, the bear went into a wallow under some alders.

Charlie shot the bear a second time, and the bear rolled into the bushes and collapsed. To make sure he was dead, the guide Charlie was hunting with tossed a stone at the grizzly's head. The bear jumped up and charged the two surprised hunters with a roar. Charlie said it was so loud it shook the ground.

The guide, who did not have his rifle with him, thought Charlie wasn't prepared to shoot again, so he took off up the mountain with the bear after him.

Just as Charlie was about to shoot again, the bear, weak from his wounds, ran back under the alders. Charlie shot it in the head. This time, they left the now-silent bear to go back down the mountain and help a second hunter skin out a bear he had taken. It would give them an opportunity to get over the scare Charlie's bear had given them.

They skinned out the other bear, and the guide sent the two hunters with the hide and skull down to the horses while he took Charlie's rifle with a couple of cartridges up to skin Charlie's bear.

The guide was cautiously walking up to the fallen grizzly when it stood up and lunged at him! The guide shot the bear in the chest and took off down the mountain, bolting the rifle with the bear on his heels, swinging its paws at him. The guide fired his second and last round over his shoulder at point-blank range. Lucky for him, this bullet broke the big grizzly's back, killing it.

I use this story to illustrate that big bears can take a lot of punishment and keep coming back for more, often when you think it's over. Most of the guides I've hunted with have a policy of putting a last bullet into the neck or spine of a big bear, even when he appears very dead.

DEALING WITH A WOUNDED BEAR

So, what do you do when you have hit a big bear that stays on his feet and makes it into thick cover?

Rule Number One: Do exactly what your guide tells you to do. You are paying him good money for his experience and knowledge, and this would be a foolish time not to follow his instructions. After all, he has probably faced this situation several times and knows what to do.

Rule Number Two: Be able to call your shots. Where did you hit the bear? How did he react as he ran off? Where did you last see him? The answers to these questions will help you and your guide determine a course of action.

Rule Number Three: Be sure to reload your rifle or handgun and put the safety on "Safe."

Rule Number Four: Wait! Give the bear an hour or so to settle down and, hopefully, die. This is difficult for some hunters to do, but it is a critical follow-up step and one that all guides recommend. If the bear is critically wounded, it won't go far. Immediate pursuit will only keep him running or create a dangerous situation for the hunter. What happens after that varies from guide to guide.

Going In

Based on the terrain, weather, shot placement, skill of the hunter and many other factors, a guide will plan the effort to get your bear as the situation dictates. Tom Rigden, a guide with whom I've enjoyed many fine bear hunts, follows these steps after waiting an appropriate length of time:

Rigden situates the hunter so that the hunter can see the guide and the area where the bear was last seen. As Rigden enters the brush, he makes sure the hunter is watching so he can alert the guide if he sees the bear.

When following a blood trail, Rigden constantly watches the surrounding brush, since bear are known to circle their quarry and attack from the rear.

If the hunter has to follow Rigden into the brush, the guide has him walk several steps behind or to one side with his rifle on "Safe," so as to create two distinct lanes of fire should the bear be encountered.

After the bear is located, dead or alive, Rigden or his hunter shoots it again to make sure. Then the guide approaches the bear with the hunter standing off to one side, ready to fire if necessary.

Expect Anything

Rigden is quick to point out that no two bears respond exactly alike when wounded, so the hunter has to expect anything. He once had a heart-stopping hunt when he was guiding a hunter for bears on the Alaska Peninsula.

Scouting revealed that a bear was feeding on a moose kill from a previous hunt. Rigden cut shooting paths in the bush around the kill so various approaches could be made to the kill, depending upon the wind conditions.

When the bear showed up again on the kill, Rigden moved his hunter to within 50 yards of the bear. With the hunter in position, Rigden began kicking brush with his feet to get the bear to move and give the hunter a better shot.

The bear stood up, and the hunter fired his .340 Wthby Mag., knocking it down. With a frightening roar, the bear got up and was shot a second time. Again he went down, but got up and ran parallel to the hunters into thick alders and cottonwoods. They waited an hour before following the bear into the dense thicket.

For a while they had a good blood trail to follow, but after a three-quarter-mile stalk, the trail ran out. Rigden realized they were playing a cat-and-mouse game with no appreciable gain, so they decided to return to camp and regroup the next morning with chief guide Brad Langvardt.

The next morning, they found a faint blood trail where they had stopped the afternoon before. The two guides spent a painstaking six hours turning over leaves, looking for the tiniest blood drop.

They had broken into a small clearing when Rigden saw a hawk land in a bush about 150 yards away. Thinking the bird might possibly be feeding on the bear carcass, he headed toward it, leaving Langvardt at the blood trail. Rigden hadn't walked 25 yards in the chest-high willows when he heard the bear roar off to his right. Shouting to Langvardt that he had heard the bear, he brought his rifle to his shoulder.

At that moment, the bear appeared at fifteen yards, staring straight at Rigden. He fired, hitting the bear just below the chin. Langvardt, only about 25 yards from the bear, also shot it, this time through the shoulders. At last, the bear was finished. The tough old bear's hide squared 10 feet 2 inches, and the skull measured 28 3/16 inches.

PREVENTION: GET CLOSE

Alaska guide Bob Hannon emphasized to me that the major reason for bears being wounded is hunters shooting at ranges greater than 100 yards. He is a firm believer in getting as close as reasonably possible to shoot.

During the years he has been guiding bear hunters, Hannon has had only eight bears wounded; just one of those got away. While he's waiting at least 45 minutes, he makes sure his rifle muzzle is free of snow, mud and other obstructions and that it is properly loaded and working. Then he positions his hunter out of the brush and uses one or two guides to follow the blood trail.

He puts one guide up front to ease along ahead of the second guide, who blood trails, and to keep a sharp look out for any sign of movement or any sound of the bear. Often on a quiet day, a wounded bear can be heard licking his wounds and even breathing. Hannon spaces his trailers five to six feet apart to keep a charging bear from hitting more than one man.

MORE CLOSE CALLS

Hannon's closest call with a wounded grizzly came when a hunter shot a bear in the hind quarter. The bear was in a creek bed adjacent to some thick willows. The hunters on a high bank could see the willows moving and hear the bear clicking his teeth just inside the brush.

After a wait, Hannon positioned his hunter on top of the high bank and proceeded to climb down into the creek bottom. Instead, he fell down the bank and rolled up to the edge of the willows. As he stopped falling, the willows next to him shook and roared. He shot three times at point-blank range. Quickly he reloaded, as the bear tried to get through the brush at him. Hannon peered through the thrashing brush and finally made out the head and neck at six feet. He shot the bear in the neck, killing it. Afterward, he learned why the bear never got him; it was broken down too badly in the hind quarters. Hannon understates, "That was some bear hunt."

Sometimes a wounded grizzly doesn't give hunters time to follow good blood-trailing practices. Once Cy Ford, a British Columbia guide with whom I've hunted, had two bear hunters in a 20-foot aluminum river boat searching for grizzlies on the Kitlope River. Near the Kitlope confluence with the Tsaytus River, they spotted a lone grizzly walking along the bank of a side channel.

Leaving one hunter with the boat, Ford took the other hunter to try to get close to the bear. At 200 yards, they saw they could get no closer. They decided to give it a try. Ford advised the hunter to wait until he had a broadside shot at the shoulder. When the grizzly turned to his right, Ford told the hunter to shoot. Just as the .300 Win. Mag. went off, the grizzly suddenly changed directions, and Ford saw the bullet hit the bear's hind leg. The grizzly went down, wallowing on the ground and bellowing madly. The hunter fired two more rounds, but Ford couldn't tell if they hit the bear. At the third shot, the bear got up and ran into the bush.

Ford then walked along the channel looking for a shallow place to wade across; the hunter followed. Just across the channel was a large patch of cottonwood trees into which the bear had disappeared at the upper end.

As Ford approached opposite the lower end of the cottonwoods, he saw the grizzly in a full charge coming right for him, quickly closing the 40-foot span. The hunter fired, but the bear continued. Ford threw up his Ruger .338 Win. Mag. and fired as the bear splashed across the channel with eyes fixed on him. The 250-grain Nosler Partition hit the bear under the chin, entering the chest cavity. Falling over backward from the shot, he drifted with the current and lodged completely under water below a log hanging off the bank.

After the dead bear was retrieved, Ford found that the hunter had hit the bear twice. Although there was a lot of blood, the grizzly hadn't been seriously hurt; it apparently felt that Ford was the cause of his aggravation and intended to do him in.

Alaska guide Larry Rivers is another believer that anything can happen when following a wounded bear. He was guiding a hunter who shot and wounded a brown bear on the coast of Alaska. They followed the wounded bear at a long distance along the rocky beach, keeping the animal in sight. Then the bear came to a high rock outcrop that blocked the beach, and he swam out into the ocean and around the rock. The hunters were unable to follow.

Disappointed, they had to abandon the bear. They started walking back along the beach to camp, but they hadn't walked far when they heard gravel falling from a high rock cliff above them. They looked up to see another brown bear some 20 feet above them. The bear charged and the hunter fired. The dead bear fell to the beach, knocking the two big-eyed men sprawling. It happened in a matter of seconds.

*This is what you **don't** want to experience on your hunt of a lifetime. Follow the shot placement guidelines in this chapter and save a pair of those expensive underwear you bought.*

BOWHUNTING A WOUNDED BEAR

The bowhunter is the most vulnerable to problems from wounded bears, since the arrow kills by hemorrhaging and doesn't usually knock a bear right down. Most successful bowhunters have to deal with a potentially still-alive bear that hasn't yet bled to death.

Jake Jacobsen, master guide and owner of Arctic Rivers Guide Service in Alaska, shared a close-call bowhunt with me. Jacobsen once had a five-day period during which his hunting clients were delayed. He and his wife watched three big caribou bulls swim across the river near their base camp. As the bulls stood on the opposite bank shaking the water off, a big grizzly rushed out of the willows and knocked one of the bulls down. It never returned to its feet. The grizzly dragged the bull into the dense willow brush.

Later that day Jacobsen flew out of camp for supplies. The next day, while preparing to land his plane back at the base camp, he saw the big grizzly sitting on his kill with

two more grizzlies nearby. That evening he decided to try to take the big bear with his bow. He had taken caribou with a bow and figured if he could get within 25 to 30 yards of the grizzly, he would have a good chance. His wife would back him up with her rifle, and he would carry a 12 gauge, .30-06 drilling slung on his back in case all else failed.

The next morning, Jacobsen and his wife started the stalk. When they got close to the caribou kill, Jacobsen told his wife to chamber a round and get ready to shoot if he yelled. He was counting on the bear being asleep, since the bear was full and wolves had barked and yipped around the kill all night.

But the bear was awake and saw the duo before they saw him. Without making a sound, the bear came at them on the run. Jacobsen said the first thing he saw was the pink inside of the bear's nose. This experienced bear hunter had an overwhelming feeling that there was going to be an accident. By reflex he drew back the bow and released the arrow.

It hit the bear in the base of the neck at an angle and penetrated to four inches from the fletching. He later learned that the broadhead had severed some major arteries and lodged in a lung.

The grizzly turned from his charge and tried to bite the arrow, Jake stuck him with a second arrow; however, it was a poor hit, as he had overdrawn. Not only that, but the overdraw cut his index finger and thumb badly, right through his glove. His wife hollered, "Jake, let's get outta here!" With his hand bleeding profusely and the grizzly thrashing wildly, he was now expecting the worst.

Dropping the bow, he shouldered the drilling. The grizzly continued to thrash about for a minute, biting at the first arrow—then fell over dead. His charge had been stopped at less than 16 feet. Had the wound been any less serious, the outcome may have been much different. This wounded bear didn't die any too soon.

At the time the bear placed sixth in the Pope and Young Club record book.

Trailing a Wounded Bear: The 10 Commandments

If the bear is wounded or if you hunt with a bow or muzzleloading rifle where death may not be instant, follow these 10 rules:

1 Check your rifle barrel with the bolt open to be sure there's no obstruction.

2 Reload immediately.

3 Be sure your firearm's action is working properly and check again to see that the gun is fully and properly loaded.

4 Wait! Give the bear 45 minutes to one hour to die or settle down. Be quiet and alert during this wait.

5 While waiting, analyze your shot placement, the bear's reaction and its exit route.

6 When the blood-trailing begins, have at least two armed hunters involved—one to watch and listen while the other follows the blood trail.

7 Stay at least six feet apart in case of a charge. This way it is more likely you both will be able to shoot.

8 Do not always assume the bear is ahead of you. It may loop off to one side and be watching his backtrail, or even stalking *you* now.

9 Be ready for anything.

10 Don't take chances. Big bears are dangerous, and rushing the trailing of a wounded bear is a mistake.

Don't rush any trailing job. If you have to go in, go in after a dead or weakened bear.

Through that season, Jacobsen had been in on the killing of 151 bears, either as hunter or guide, and had only been charged 12 times. Of these, eight were wounded bears, two were grizzlies on kills, one was a sow with cubs and one was unprovoked.

BLOOD TRAILING

There is no precise procedure for blood-trailing a wounded bear, as there is for white-tailed deer. I have seen bears that lost a good bit of blood survive without any difficulty and some which lost little blood but were found dead. The fat and long hair on the bears often cause the blood trail to be faint.

Guides who hunt most of their bears when snow is on the ground seem to have the best percentage of recovering wounded bears. The faintest blood trail is easy to follow, and the crippled bear has a tough time getting away in deep snow.

The potential danger of trailing a wounded bear cannot be over-emphasized. I have talked to the survivors of two wounded-bear hunts in which the bear killed one of the hunters, and it was a tragedy for both the victim and the survivors.

Many dead bears have been found in a position which afforded them an ambush should anyone have been on their backtrail. Their last instinct was to confront the cause of their pain.

TAKE ENOUGH SHOTS

There should never be a bear wounded and lost by a modern rifle or handgun hunter. If the big bear hunter will work hard to get within 100 yards of an unsuspecting bear, pick his target well and place his shot through the shoulders, the bear will be anchored. Then the second and, if necessary, third shots should be driven through the shoulder/lung area. As Larry Rivers puts it, "There should be no one-shot bear." This is not the time for an ego trip.

Shot Placement

Chapter Eight

AVOIDING BEAR PROBLEMS

*T*he only close encounter you want with a brown, grizzly or polar bear is walking up to a stone-dead animal with a feeling of great accomplishment welling up within you, and your guide slapping you on the back. What you don't want is this: Getting involved with some belligerent bear that's raiding your camp or getting into your food and ready for a fight with those irritating little beings (you and the other humans around) trying to break up the party. Here's how to avoid those confrontations.

AVOIDING BEAR PROBLEMS

M ost bear-caused deaths and maulings do not occur when the hunter shoots a bear; they usually occur in camp or when people are walking in big bear country.

THE THOMPSONS' STORY

One of the most publicized bear maulings I know of occurred many years ago, when Alaska game warden Al Thompson and his wife backpacked into the Kenai National Moose Range to bowhunt for moose. Thompson also carried his .44 Mag. handgun, and his wife took her .30-06. Their camp was a comfortable lean-to made of poles and plastic.

On the second night of their hunt, Thompson was awakened at 3:30 a.m. by a sense that something was wrong. He woke his wife and told her to stay still and that something was outside. As Thompson reached for the rifle, an enraged grizzly came through the top of the lean-to. Knocking the rifle from Thompson's hand, the bear tried to tear Mrs. Thompson from her sleeping bag. Thompson hit the bear with his hand, and the bear turned on him. There was no time to grab the pistol. The bear snatched his left arm and flung him across the lean-to. Next, it grabbed Thompson's scalp with its mouth, picking him up and running out of the lean-to. The bear's front paw ripped a gash in Thompson's chest.

After carrying Thompson 80 feet, the bear dropped him. Thompson knew that he would have to play dead with his belly down if he was to survive.

His left arm useless, he used his right arm to position himself belly down and held his breath until he almost passed out. The bear chewed on Thompson's back and hit the side of his head with his claws as the man played dead. Abruptly, the bear left.

The rest of the story is a credit to both Thompson and his wife, as they had to walk out some 15 miles to get help. Thompson survived, but it was a long battle to recovery.

BEARS IN CAMP

Alaska guide Larry Rivers tells two interesting accounts of bears coming into hunting camps.

Once, his wife heard their dog barking, and she stepped out of the cook tent to see the dog half in and half out of the family tent, where their daughter was asleep. The dog was barking at a grizzly only about three yards away. Mrs. Rivers picked up some stones and threw them at the bear. The bear ran out of camp down to the edge of a nearby river, where he proceeded to consume the groceries that were in the river to be kept cool.

Next, the bear stomped up and down the river's edge. Then the bear charged back into camp, and Mrs. Rivers, with shotgun in hand, threw a stick at the bear, causing him to run back to the river. Reaching the river, the bear turned and once again charged into camp straight at Mrs. Rivers. She was forced to shoot when the bear got within 20 feet. One charge of 00 buckshot killed the bear.

On another occasion, Rivers had two guides and two hunters in a spike camp, which had a four-man tent suspended from an exterior frame with elastic cord. One night a brown bear sow with three cubs came into camp and rather enjoyed, much to the horror of the tent's occupants, putting their feet up on the tent, pushing it down, and then letting it spring back up. This went on for two to three hours.

Once a cub annoyed its mother, and she slapped it into the tent's side. At daybreak, one of the guides unzipped the tent door some four inches at the bottom to look out. As he bent down to look out, with the three other hunters also trying to get a peek, the sow stuck her nose through the opening. Instantly, the previously crowded tent had plenty of room around the door.

Soon after that, the bear left them and the hunters moved their camp about a quarter mile, hoping to have some peace that night. But it was not to be, as that night, the same bear came into the new campsite to play with the tent again. This time, one of the guides decided to shoot his .338 Win. Mag. with the muzzle next to the sow's head in hopes it would scare the bear away. Sticking the rifle barrel only 18 inches away from the sow's head, the guide fired into the air. The old sow never blinked an eye. Once again, the bear started playing on the tent. It was another long night.

RULE ONE: DON'T SET UP NEAR THE BEARS

The first rule in avoiding bear problems in camp is to not set up camp in a place that forces bears to

The one place where a bear hunter doesn't want to encounter a bear is in camp, but it does happen to sloppy hunting camps.

move through a small area. Don't set up camp on or adjacent to a bear trail. Avoid sites where roaring streams drown out sounds; bears that hear you will usually avoid you. Also, don't camp near bear feeding sites, such as berry patches and salmon spawning areas.

Be sure to plan your camp carefully, especially if it is a base camp. Keep sleeping tents together, separate from the kitchen and food storage areas. The sleeping tent should be upwind of the cook tent. Evening winds usually blow down valley. Clear out all underbrush and branches around camp below four or five feet for better visibility along the ground.

RULE TWO: BEAR-PROOF YOUR FOOD

Perhaps the most important rule is to make all food storage bear-proof, either by suspending it from a tree out of reach of bears or in food storage con-

tainers made from metal drums.

One of the most frightening nights I ever spent in a hunting camp was in a camp with cabins made from logs with a tent top. There were two cabins in camp: a cook cabin with a large picnic table in it, where all cooking and eating took place, and a sleeping cabin, where guides and hunters slept. Since the cook had to get up so early each morning to prepare breakfast on time, he slept on the large table in the cook cabin.

One night we were all awakened by the sounds of splintering wood and the cook screaming. Then there were five shots from the cook cabin. The cook hollered for us not to come out, that a bear had torn the door off its hinges and gotten in the cabin with him. The cook, who had managed to leap off the table while still in his sleeping bag, grabbed a shotgun loaded with slugs and emptied it into the bear at arm's length.

We shined a bright flashlight over on the cook tent doorway to see the big-eyed cook sticking his head out, trying to reload the shotgun. No one slept, thinking the wounded bear was just outside our camp. The next morning, we found the bear dead a few yards from the cook tent.

RULE THREE: KEEP A CLEAN CAMP

Keeping a clean camp can go a long way toward avoiding bear trouble. All dishes should be washed after meals. Food garbage should be burned. Horse pellets and strong-smelling plastics and lubricants should be stored like food and away from camp. Daypacks should be checked when returning to camp to discard food leftovers.

I credit a clean camp for preventing another hunter and me from having major bear problems. We were stranded near the Yukon-British Columbia line with little camp gear except our two-man mountain tent and sleeping bags. The only food we had for days was trout we caught from the lake where our survival camp was located.

Bear sign was all around, and we took great pains to sink all trout scraps, including the sticks we cooked them on, out in the lake. It was a good thing,

Proper food storage, like this suspended cache, will go a long way toward avoiding camp bears.

for each night a grizzly would come into camp, even with a campfire burning near the door of our small tent, and sniff around the tent. It was awesome to lie in the tent and see its walls shake from the bear's breath and hear him sniff all around the edges. He never caused a problem other than a loss of sleep.

WHAT TO DO

If you should encounter a bear, stay calm, as it will probably leave you alone once it gets your scent. Don't make abrupt moves or noises that would startle the bear. Give it plenty of room.

Slowly detour, keeping upwind so it will get your scent and know you are there. If you cannot detour, look for a tree to climb while waiting for the bear to move away. Most grizzlies won't climb a tree after you, but some have been known to climb right behind a man if the limbs are close together.

A clean camp can prevent major bear problems. Bears don't explore camps where food and trash are not available.

Avoiding Bears: Some Tips

One way you can keep most bears out of camp is to urinate at different locations around the camp. Of course, this can foul up your hunting around the camp, especially downwind.

When camping in small tents, it is a good idea to keep a sharp knife handy so that you can create a door if necessary. Also, it's wise in any camp to keep a bright flashlight and your rifle handy. Some grizzly and brown bear guides keep dogs in camp as an early warning of bears. The sled dogs used on polar bear hunts serve this same purpose.

Always carry your rifle with you when leaving the immediate camp area to go down to a stream, to take a hike or to go to the bathroom.

Be sure to hang game meat out of the reach of bears.

If you are hiking around camp, be sure to make plenty of noise so as not to surprise a bear. All bears have a certain critical space. If you surprise a bear within that range, anything can happen. Don't try to slip up on a bear to take photographs, or worse yet, feed the bear. If you ever have to enter a thicket, do it from upwind so your smell will warn any bears of your presence.

Avoiding Bear Problems

A Charging Bear

Most bears don't charge, but some will, sometimes for no apparent reason. If one should charge, your options are:

- Climb a stout tree.
- Drop a pack or coat to distract the bear while you ease off.
- Shoot the bear, making sure your first shot either breaks his shoulders or enters the brain.
- If unarmed, assume a cannonball position to protect your head and stomach while playing dead.

The one option you don't have is to run. Amazing as it may seem, big bears can attain a burst of speed up to 40 miles per hour in seconds. Also, it is instinctive for them to chase running animals.

AN UNPREDICTABLE ANIMAL

As has been reiterated many times (with good reason) in this book: big bears are unpredictable. Their reasons for attacking are many. A bear may attack if it considers you a threat. A polar bear may consider you a meal. You may get too close to a bear or to cubs, startle it or run up on a bear that has been beaten up by another bear or had a previous run-in with a person. It could be injured, or it could just be one of those attacks for which there is no apparent explanation.

Since in all likelihood your bear hunts and most other hunts conducted in big bear country will be guided, you will be under the watchful eye of a professional who knows how to avoid bear problems. By following his rules, you probably won't have any trouble.

More outdoorsmen are hurt and killed each year by poisonous snakes, lightning and many other acts of nature than by all bears, so the risk is not great ... *if* you take the proper precautions.

When you come fact to face with a bear, the one certain thing is that you don't know what he will do. Be ready.

A charging bear can run as fast as a horse. You cannot outrun him, so don't try. This is an Alaska brown bear on Kodiak Island.

Chapter Nine

BEAR TROPHIES

Any and every brown, grizzly or polar bear is the trophy of a lifetime ... it does not matter how many inches of skull or feet of hide or pounds of bear are there. The real trophy lies in hunting well, making a clean kill, and living to tell about it all until you're old and gray. But because we are human, there are some numbers attached to the harvest of these great animals, and those concerns are outlined here, along with other important insights into making sure your animal is cared for and processed properly so your trophy is as beautiful and memorable as the hunt that produced it.

JUDGING TROPHY BEARS

Any legally harvested polar, grizzly or brown bear is certainly a trophy to the hunter who brings the animal down in a sporting manner. Due to the nature of big bear hunting, we don't always have the opportunity to pick and choose our bears. However, most of us would like to take a bear that is really considered big. In many cases, it is simply luck if a trophy-sized bear is taken, but sometimes other factors come together and give you the opportunity to look at several bears from which to choose.

FIELD JUDGING

Big bears are among the most difficult animals to judge in the field. To most hunters, they all look big. Alaska guide Larry Rivers says there is no substitute for experience in field-judging bears. He and his assistant guides study the valleys they hunt in and learn the size of reference points, such as cut banks, rocks, etc. Then when they see a bear out at a distance, they compare it in size to one of the known reference points at a similar distance. In open country, it is even harder to judge the distance. Is it a big bear far away or a small bear fairly close? For accurate distance judging, a rangefinder can be helpful.

Tracks

If he is tracking a bear, Rivers measures the distance across the pad of one of the bear's front feet in the tracks. To that he adds one inch. That number of inches is generally equal to the number of feet the bear's hide will square. For instance, if the bear's footprint is seven inches across the pad, the bear hide will proba-

around eight feet. This doesn't hold true all the time, but it's a good rule of thumb to use in the field.

Rivers also points out that if you ask yourself, "I wonder if that's a big bear?" when watching a bear, he probably isn't very big. But if your initial reaction is, "That's a huge bear," he probably is. But be aware that big bears look big to those who have seen few bears.

Look at the Walk

Other rules of thumb used by guides when judging bears include one which considers how the bear walks. Very large bears walk with a swinging waddle, and small bears walk with no waddle or movement in the rear.

Some guides say they judge a bear by its legs. If

To estimate the length of the bear that made this track, measure the distance across the pad and add one inch: A pad with a seven-inch width was made by an approximately eight-foot bear.

they appear to be very short with the body close to the ground, it is a large bear. If the legs appear to be long with the body high, it is a small bear. Guide David O'Keeffe describes a large bear as looking like a mule without legs.

A guide I worked with in British Columbia judges his bears by their ears. If the ears appear to be small and stick out of the side of the head, it is usually a large bear. If the ears are easily seen and stick out the top of the head, it is a small bear.

Since chances are good you will be hunting with a guide who knows what a really big bear looks like, you won't have to know any special tricks for field-judging bears. Unfortunately, many hunters do not find enough bears to be too picky. It takes some luck to get a high-scoring bear.

If the bear you're looking at has a small head, short legs, and a body close to the ground, he's a very large bear!

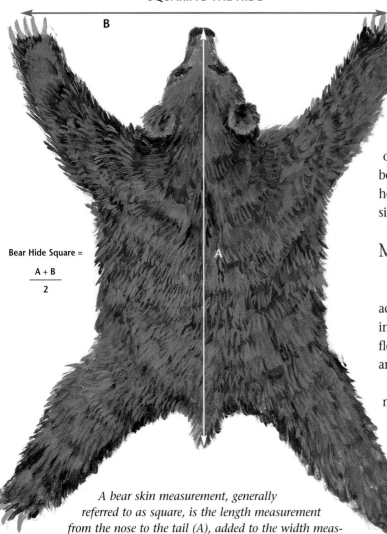

B

A

Bear Hide Square =

$$\frac{A + B}{2}$$

A bear skin measurement, generally referred to as square, is the length measurement from the nose to the tail (A), added to the width measurement from claw tip to claw tip of the front legs (B), divided by two.

SQUARING THE HIDE

Harvested bears are evaluated in two ways: by squaring the hide and by measuring the skull.

Here's how to square a hide. First lay the fresh skin out flat. Using a measuring tape, measure from the end of its nose to the end of its tail, not counting hair. Then, without moving the hide, measure from the end of the claws on one front foot to the end of the claws on the other front foot. Add the two measurements and divide the total by two. You have the square measurement.

Big inland grizzlies will square up to eight feet or so, coastal grizzlies and browns will square up to about 10 feet, and polar bears up to about 11 feet. A brown or grizzly hide may be as wide as it is long,

while a polar bear hide is long and narrow.

You can see that this is a general method of earning bragging rights, and the unscrupulous guide or hunter can easily stretch the green hide to obtain exaggerated numbers. I once watched two hunters pull and tug on a green grizzly hide, to the point of almost pulling off one of the front legs where several bullets had hit the bear, to get a high squared measurement. But if done honestly and correctly, squaring is a good method of sizing up a bear.

MEASURING THE SKULL

The method of scoring a trophy bear that is accepted by most trophy records programs is measuring a clean, dry skull. Notice I said clean and dry: All flesh, cartilage and membrane must be off the skull, and the skull allowed to dry for at least 60 days.

A caliper is needed to measure the skull. Two measurements are taken with the caliper, each to the nearest one-sixteenth of an inch. The first measurement is the longest length, from the forward tip of the skull to the rear of the skull.

The second measurement is the widest point of the skull. These two measurements are added to give the score.

Not only is the skull a real and honest means of trophy scoring, but a bleached skull on a plaque makes a nice trophy display.

Several hunting organizations have hunter recognition awards for hunters taking trophy-class bears.

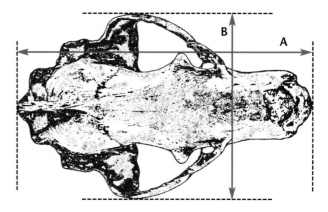

B

A

To score a bear skull, measure the longest (A) and widest (B) points, and add the two numbers together.

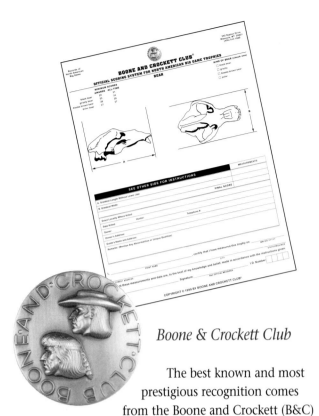

Boone & Crockett Club

The best known and most prestigious recognition comes from the Boone and Crockett (B&C) Club. B&C has kept a record book on North American big game since 1932, and most of us hunters would like to have a trophy animal "in the book," a term referring to the B&C record book. Its scoring techniques are simple and fair, and are used by many other organizations for trophy rating. B&C only accepts the measurements of one of its trained official measurers.

For their record book, B&C has a separate category for the big coastal brown bear and the interior grizzly. A line of separation between the larger-growing coastal brown bear and the smaller interior grizzly has been developed such that west and south of this line (to and including Unimak Island), bear trophies are recorded as Alaska brown bears. North and east of this line, bear trophies are recorded as grizzly bears.

The boundary line is described as follows: Starting at Pearse Canal and following the Canada-Alaska boundary northwesterly to Mt. St. Elias on the 141-degree meridian; thence north along the Canada-Alaska boundary to Mt. Natazhat; thence north along the divide of the Mentasta Range to Mt. Mentasta Pass; thence in a general westerly direction along the divide of the Alaska Range to Houston Pass; thence westerly following the 62nd parallel of latitude to the Bering Sea.

Polar bears must be taken in either U.S.- or Canadian-held water or land mass in order to be eligible. However, the record book is closed to new polar bear entries at this time because of the Marine Mammal Protection Act.

Minimum scores for entering trophy bears into the B&C all-time record book are: brown bears—28; grizzly bears—24; and polar bears—27. At this writing, the record for each bear is as follows: brown—$30^{12}/16$, taken on Kodiak Island, Alaska; grizzly—$27^2/16$, taken on Dean River, British Columbia; polar—$29^{15}/16$, taken near Kotzebue, Alaska.

North American Hunting Club

The North American Hunting Club has an annual hunter recognition program called the Big Game Awards for which members send in a photo and an official Club scoresheet. Entries are judged on their score and on the location of the hunt compared to the entries from other members. Recognition is given for each species taken in four hunting categories: bow, rifle, handgun and muzzleloader. Prizes are also awarded randomly, allowing all entrants a chance to win valuable prizes.

The NAHC President's Trophy is given to the member selected by a panel of judges, who had the most challenging hunt, although not necessarily the largest animal. The hunt is judged based on quality and difficulty of the hunting experience.

Pope & Young Club

The Pope and Young (P&Y) Club is the official record-keeping organization for trophies taken by bowhunters.

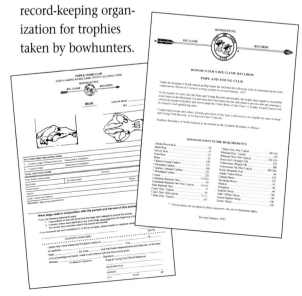

P&Y uses the same scoring system as B&C, with lower minimum entrance levels for each game species in consideration of the added difficulty in taking an exceptional animal by bow. Like B&C, P&Y has trained official measurers throughout North America. Trophies that score high enough may be entered in both the P&Y and B&C record books.

Minimum scores for inclusion in the P&Y book are: grizzly—19; polar—20; brown—20. At this writing, the number one bears are: grizzly—25^{13}/16, a tie between two British Columbia bears; polar—26^6/16, taken on Cape Lisburne in Alaska; brown—28^7/16, taken on Unimak Island in Alaska, with another taken at Ursus Cove, Alaska.

The Longhunter

The youngest of the major big game records programs was established by the National Muzzle Loading Rifle Association. Designed to recognize trophies taken by muzzleloading hunters, it is called The Longhunter.

The name "Longhunter" was chosen to honor those hunters/explorers who pushed across the Appalachian Mountains into the vast, unexplored land we now call Kentucky and Tennessee. Often alone, occasionally in small groups, they penetrated a virtually unknown wilderness.

The name "Longhunter" was appropriate, for their journeys often lasted more than a year and were punctuated by solitude, hos-

tile Indians, shelter under overhanging rocks and a diet consisting only of what the land provided.

The Longhunter also follows the B&C method of scoring big game trophies. The trophy must be taken with a muzzleloading firearm and rules of fair chase must be followed.

Minimum scores for bears to be listed in the record book are: grizzly—19; brown—21; and polar—22. At this writing, the top record for each bear is as follows: brown—26^{15}/16, taken in Portage Bay, Alaska; and grizzly—23^2/16, taken in the Brooks Range of Alaska. Since this is a fairly young program, there are currently no polar bear entries.

Safari Club International

The Safari Club International offers its members a trophy recognition program which includes a record book. Its scoring method on bears is the same as the B&C. Minimum scores for inclusion are: grizzly—22; brown—25; and polar—26.

Safari Club International has designated brown and grizzly bear territories as follows: Bears taken within 75 miles of tidewater south of Nome are classed as Alaska brown bears. Bears taken more than 75 miles from tidewater south of Nome, and taken north of Nome, are classed as grizzly bears.

PRESERVING YOUR TROPHY BEAR

A while back I was in a taxidermy shop when the owner had to break the news to a hunter that his guide hadn't taken proper care of his brown bear skin and that it was ruined. I thought I was going to see a grown man cry. He had invested $11,500 in his hunting trip, not to mention two years' worth of vacation time he had saved up for the hunt. Now all he had was a skull and a few pictures that weren't very good.

BEAR SKINS

For many hunters, a big bear is a once-in-a-lifetime trophy that is taken at great expense in time, money and effort. It behooves all hunters to know something about the proper way a bear skin should be preserved in the field.

Identify Your Taxidermist

The first step to take in making sure you will get a good trophy mount is to select the best taxidermist you can *before* you leave for your hunt. Find a taxidermist who frequently works with big bears.

Look at samples of the taxidermist's bear mounts and examine them for small details. Pay close attention to the work around the eyes and ears. Look for small splits or unnatural appearances. Examine the

work around the mouth and feet. Ask your prospective taxidermist for references, some who have bear mounts that are several years old. Go see those mounts and find out if the owners are happy with his work.

Don't expect a good taxidermist to be cheap. He is a skilled artist and craftsman, and as with most things in life, you get what you pay for. At this writing, a full body mount on a big bear will cost from $2,000 to $4,000, and bear rugs are priced beginning at $100 per running foot.

Talk with Your Taxidermist

Once you select a taxidermist, let him know your bear hunt plans and desires for a trophy mount. He can be helpful as you decide how you want your bear mounted. With this decided, be sure you get from the taxidermist any special instructions he has for you to use on your hunt. For instance, many taxidermists who are going to do a full body mount on big bears want the bear's measurements before he is skinned. The taxidermist may want measurements from the tip of the nose to the root of the tail, the height at the shoulders, circumference of the body behind the front legs and in the middle of the body, circumference of the neck and other measurements.

Also, ask your taxidermist about field care and about shipping the skin and hide to him. A good taxidermist can be a big help in planning your trophy care.

SKINNING ADVICE

Bud Jones is a Georgia taxidermist who has mounted many big bears. He says that most guides are reliable and know how to properly handle bear skins, but often a new guide or one who is in a big

Take care of your bear skin soon after the harvest, especially in warm weather, to prevent the hair from slipping.

hurry will do a poor job of skinning, fleshing and salting. Then the hunter winds up with a ruined trophy. During one spring, Jones got three beautiful bear skins from one guide who didn't turn the ears when he salted the skins, and all of the hair fell off the ears.

Another well-known bear taxidermist, Joel Stone, says he has seen the same problems. Stone said that because of the fat content in a bear, its hair will slip faster after death than that of any other animal. The hair is released from the skin due to the action of bacteria which start growing as soon as the bear dies. The more moist and warm the skin, the faster the hair slips. For this reason, a bear should be skinned as quickly as possible after the pictures and any necessary measurements have been taken.

Salt It Well

Both taxidermists told me that the hunter should be sure there is plenty of salt in the bear camp. If there is any doubt, the hunter should take 50 to 100 pounds of salt per bear. I have to agree with this, as I have been on several hunts when the guide ran out of salt because of poor planning, rain getting into the bags of salt, more animals than expected being taken or a trip back for supplies not taking place for some reason. A few dollars for extra salt is good

insurance for your trophy.

Common table salt is the best type. The finer the salt the better, as fine grains can be rubbed into tight places that rock salt or ice cream salt can't. Some guides use the coarser types, and I make it a point to ask about this before I go on my hunt. If they do use coarse salt, I offer to pay the price of their having fine salt for my skins.

Skinning Procedure

Since most bears are to be made into rugs or mounted life-size, the skinning procedure is the same.

With the bear on its back, a cut is made in the skin from the center of the throat to the end of the tail. From this line, cut down each leg all the way to the pad. Some bear skinners want to cut the pads off, but you should insist that they don't, especially if the bear is to be mounted life-size. Skin out the feet to the last joints, leaving the claws attached to the

Don't Wash It!

According to the taxidermists I've talked to, a few guides will want to wash a bear skin in water or in a brine solution. Don't do it: Water and moisture are a skin's worst enemy. Don't worry about any mud and dirt in the hair; your taxidermist can take care of that when he gets the skin.

hide. The remainder of the job is to remove the skin from the carcass with a sharp knife, leaving as much fat and tissue on the carcass as possible. A good job of skinning can save a lot of work fleshing.

Fleshing

When the bear is skinned, the next step is for all fat and tissue to be fleshed from the skin. A good fleshing job is the mark of a good guide. The ears should be turned, the lips and nose should be split, and the pads should be left on but fleshed on the inside. This is so that salt can be hand-rubbed into all of these areas.

How to Salt the Skins

Once the fleshing is complete, rub salt over the inside of the skin. Use a lot of salt. You can't use too much, and not using enough will ruin your skin.

Make sure it gets into every crack and crevice. All bullet holes should be well salted. Salt pulls out all the moisture in which the bacteria thrive, so your goal is to completely dry the skin by using salt.

A mistake many hunters make when all of this is going on is celebrating success by the fire rather than watching to make sure their guide or his helper is doing a thorough job of fleshing and salting the skin. This is not the time to turn your back on your trophy. On more hunts than I care to talk about I have had to get involved in the salting process in order to get a good coat of salt on the skin.

Hang & Stretch

Once a heavy coat of salt is placed on the skin, it is best to hang the skin, stretched out, so that the moisture being drained from the skin can run off. Be sure the freshly salted skin is not exposed to the sun, a camp stove or campfire. Keep it cool and in the shade. Be sure animals such as porcupines can't get to the skin; they like salt.

One day later, the guide should remove the salt, then resalt the skin, taking the same care to get clean salt into every crack and crease. Watch for folds or wrinkles in the skin, as they are often overlooked when salting, and this can result in hair slipping. Be sure all the edges of the skin are well-salted.

SKULL CARE

While the skin is being salted, the bear skull should have all the meat cut off and then it should be boiled in water to remove the remaining tissue. Once the skull is tissue-free and is removed from the hot water, a wire hook made from a coat hanger or a

Removing all the flesh from the skull and the brains is a lot of work, but the skull will make an impressive trophy.

green stick should be used to pull the remaining brain tissue out through the opening where the spine joined the skull.

PACKING & SHIPPING

When it is time to return home, you should have a burlap bag, or as Joel Stone recommends, an army surplus canvas duffel bag in which to pack your dried bear skin. Since it should be dry, there is no need to pack it in anything waterproof, such as a plastic garbage bag, as this can cause heat to build up and start bacterial action again.

Keep your bear tag and any other necessary paperwork with your bear skin. While there are no current restrictions on traveling with grizzly or brown bear skins, you should be able to prove it is a legal harvest at any time the skin is en route. Be sure to check current regulations *prior to* booking your hunt.

Once you get home, get your bear skin to your taxidermist immediately; don't put it off. If you have to ship it, call to let the taxidermist know that it's on the way and when it will arrive. I always put my bear skins in a freezer if there is any delay while traveling home or getting the skin to my taxidermist.

I have stored bear skins in freezers at airports

Hard Work

*P*acking out a fresh grizzly or brown bear skin that may weigh from 80 to 150 pounds is no easy task. This, along with caring properly for the skin, should earn your guide a healthy tip.

where an overnight stop was necessary. Just tell an airline representative what you need and you will usually be pointed in the right direction. I have stored skins in hotel freezers and once talked a restaurant in Vancouver, British Columbia, into letting me put a grizzly skin and skull in their freezer. I got some strange looks, but they agreed to it at no cost.

When the big day finally arrives and you get a call from your taxidermist to pick up your trophy, ask for information on care and cleaning of the trophy. With proper care and an occasional cleaning, it will be in your trophy room as a reminder of a great hunt, for the rest of your life.

Bear Trophies

Chapter Ten

THE FUTURE

*P*erhaps no other North American game animal is as inextricably tied to real wilderness as are brown, grizzly and polar bears. Of course, they need big country, wild country—and lots of it—to make a living. But they also need all that space to be separated from human habitation and its negative effects on bear habitat and habits. To love our big bears means to love some of the last truly wild places on earth; do what you can to preserve them both.

Looking at the Resource

Big Bears in the Lower 48

Polar, brown and grizzly bears are truly animals of the wilderness, and as man and his activities encroach on the rapidly diminishing wild areas of North America, these bears pay the price. This has been seen dramatically in the lower 48 states.

When the first European explorers entered the western half of the United States, they found grizzlies in parts of what have become 17 western states. It has been estimated that as many as 100,000 grizzlies called this area home. Truthfully, we have no way of determining an accurate number, but we do know that the population was substantial. In 1824, a Kentuckian named James Ohio Pattie led an expedition into the southwestern part of the country. During one day of travel along the Arkansas River, he recorded seeing 220 grizzlies.

Beginning with the early fur traders, bear numbers declined where man and bears lived in the same area. This decline was partly due to the indiscriminate killing of the big animals as pests. However, other factors played a major role in this decline, including loss of habitat to farms and ranches, reduction of prey, and an increase of mining, timber cutting, railroad construction and predator control.

The grizzly had disappeared from the West Coast beaches by the 1870s, the prairie river bottoms in the 1880s, open mountain valleys by 1899 and most foothill areas by 1915. Grizzlies were last seen in Texas in 1890, North Dakota in 1897, California in 1922, Utah in 1923, Oregon and New Mexico in 1931, Arizona in 1935 and Colorado in 1979. Grizzlies, retreating from the urbanization of the West, are now found in only six areas, within which

there remain fewer than 1,000. There is no grizzly bear hunting in the Lower 48.

The best known of these grizzly environments is the Yellowstone ecosystem. This area includes Yellowstone National Park, Grand Teton National Park and five surrounding national forests, for a total of four million acres. It has been estimated that 250 to 350 grizzlies remain in the area.

The Northern Continental Divide ecosystem encompasses Glacier National Park and the wilderness areas and associated lands south to the Blackfoot drainage and northwest to the Kootenai drainage. It is difficult to estimate bear numbers in this area, as it joins Canada's Waterton National Park

The Future

and vast forest lands in Alberta and British Columbia.

The Cabinet Yaak ecosystem contains some 1,800 square miles in the northwest corner of Montana. It is estimated that only about 25 grizzlies are in that area.

On the Montana-Idaho line is the Bitterroot-Selway ecosystem, which is in part of America's largest mountainous wilderness below Alaska. This ecosystem is in the Bitterroot Mountains and associated wilderness lands north to the Salmon River and west to the Selway drainage in northcentral Idaho. It is not known how many grizzlies live in this vast area.

The Selkirk Mountains ecosystem is located in the Selkirk Mountains in northeast Washington and the panhandle of Idaho. Between 12 and 40 grizzlies live in that ecosystem.

In western Washington is the North Cascades ecosystem, located in the northern edge of the Cascade Mountains. Few grizzlies remain in this scenic country.

The outlook for grizzly hunting in the Lower 48 is uncertain for the foreseeable future. While bear populations are on the rebound, most ecosystems simply do not have huntable populations. Some of the most populous areas are within national parks, and, of course, no hunting is allowed there.

It has taken a long time for funds to become available and wildlife management techniques to be developed to conduct in-depth bear studies and management. This has now come about, and work is currently being done to help save the grizzly. This effort will likely face an uphill battle, as so much is being done in the name of progress and recreation that is counter-productive to grizzly habitat and behavior. Those of us who want to hunt grizzlies will have to look north for the years ahead, keeping in mind that the same thing that has happened to the grizzly in the Lower 48 could happen in Canada and Alaska as well.

THE OUTLOOK IN CANADA

Fortunately, the big bears have fared much better in Canada than in the United States. While habitat destruction and abuse of the grizzly have occurred in some locales, a lot of bear hunting is left. Thanks to the research and management practices followed by the various Canadian wildlife agencies, the grizzly is holding his own in many areas.

Best-known for big coastal grizzlies and many interior grizzlies is British Columbia. While the province doesn't have as large a number of bears in some areas as it once had due to the influence of man's heavy hand, the population is estimated at 5,000 to 8,000 grizzlies. The outlook is good for the future. Most of the guides in British Columbia have exclusive guiding rights to a specific area, and the ones I've hunted with do a good job of taking care of the bears in their area. Future bear hunting, and in turn the guide's future income, depend on it.

The Yukon has a grizzly population estimated at 5,000 animals, and the population seems to be stable. I am told that

Bears are animals of the wilderness. Future development of public lands must be minimal if bear populations are to remain at a healthy level.

slightly more than half of the grizzly quota is being harvested, so this means a lot of mature bears are available. If the bear situation in the Yukon has a problem in the future, it is likely to be from mineral development. This activity is on the increase, and is opening access to some remote areas. This could lead to a decline in grizzly numbers.

Alberta has had some trophy-class bears taken in the past, but like the Lower 48, the province has seen some big changes in bear population. At the present, the grizzly population is estimated at 800 animals. Most of these bears are found along the western border, especially in the areas of Jasper and Banff National Parks. Grizzly hunting is now controlled through a limited entry draw available only to residents.

The Northwest Territories is a vast land with few people, and because so much of it is uninhabited, any grizzly population estimate is just a guess. Several areas, primarily in the western and northwestern sections of the territory, do have huntable populations, and grizzly biologists there say the population appears to be stable. This is one area that is looking up for grizzly hunters, as nonresidents are now permitted to hunt in a few areas on a limited basis. Next door, in the relatively new Canadian province of Nunavut, barren ground grizzlies can be hunted, but only on permits purchased from native hunting guides.

With good management and protection of habitat, your children and grandchildren should be able to experience the adventure of a big bear hunt.

ALASKA

The brightest grizzly hunting outlook comes from Alaska. Alaska's brown and grizzly population is currently estimated at between 32,000 and 43,000 animals. Biologists' field reports confirm that bear populations in Alaska continue to appear healthy and abundant.

Alaska has a good bear management program, and prospects for the future, at least on the surface, appear to be very good. However, there are many factors beyond sport hunting and bear management that can and do have a major impact on brown and grizzly bears. The same factors which almost wiped out the grizzly in the Lower 48 are at play in Alaska.

Livestock production, agriculture, mining, industrial expansion, urban expansion, homesteading, oil exploration, hydroelectric production and general road construction are all counter-productive to the well-being of big bears. Alaska is a state receiving much attention from all of these interests, and sportsmen, as well as wildlife planners, must be involved in the long-range planning for growth in this state if the bear situation is to remain as good as it is at present.

Unrestricted hunting by native claims, bear/man confrontations by recreationists and defense-of-life-or-property kills will also play major roles in the future of the bears.

We are fortunate that Alaska is still made up mostly of federal lands, which gives the sportsmen a say-so in planning; however, there is a potential danger built in, as public lands are managed by bureaucrats who are often more involved with the mechanics of politics than in doing a good job with sound planning for the future of wildlife management. A federal and/or state administration with strong leanings toward development of our federal lands could destroy the brown and grizzly populations in a relatively short period.

While we enjoy the good hunting in Alaska now, let's remember what happened to the big bears in the Lower 48 and make sure the same thing doesn't occur in the 49th state.

POLAR BEAR OUTLOOK

Polar bears in North America cover a vast range, extending from Newfoundland and James Bay northward 2,000 miles and laterally across the Arctic some 2,700 miles. This includes the northern coast of Alaska, the Yukon, Northwest Territories and Nunavut, as well as the provinces along the Hudson Bay.

Until the enactment of the Marine Mammal

Polar bear populations in North America are at good levels and the large bear's future remains bright.

Protection Act, Alaska offered excellent polar bear hunting to those who could afford the two ski-equipped planes usually used in this sport. It was very risky hunting, and more often than once, guides and hunters disappeared or got into serious trouble out on the ice pack.

It was not a declining population of polar bears in North America that brought about the Marine Mammal Protection Act. Instead, it was the unlimited hunting for hides in Russia that necessitated the act. As a result, all hunting of polar bears was stopped in Alaska except that done by Native peoples, and they cannot sell the hides. At this writing, the only polar bear hunting available in North America is that offered by some native villages in Canada's Northwest Territories. Hunts there must be conducted by dogsled, and the hides can (at this writing) be brought into the United States. The hunts are expensive and extremely demanding, both physically and mentally.

The polar bear population in North America is at a healthy number, according to wildlife biologists. The number is impossible to determine, as these animals range far and wide. The worldwide population has been estimated at 15,000. Currently, the annual harvest in North America is about 600, with the vast majority of those taken by natives for food, clothing and dog food. A few are killed around oil drilling camps and other populated areas as self-protection.

The future of hunting polar bears remains uncertain. Several hunting organizations are working toward getting Alaska reopened for sport hunting, since it is well established that the bear population could withstand regulated hunting pressure.

While the North American polar bear population seems secure at this time, many factors will determine its numbers in the future. Since the polar bear diet is comprised mainly of seals, any decline in the seal population affects the bear population. Another factor that could affect the polar bear is climatic change, such as a warming trend in the Arctic. Also,

the threat from water pollution becomes more serious every year.

Like the environment of all big bears, the polar bear's habitat must be watched carefully.

A FINAL NOTE

The future of all the big bears rests in the hands of man. If we are to continue to have huntable populations, certain concessions must be made by land managers, developers, public land administrators, politicians and everyone else who affects bear habitat. We are fortunate to have the number of big bears we have, but unfortunately, we probably can't expect to see much increase in these numbers in the future.

We hunters can do much toward keeping the big bears at their current level though. We can suggest land use that favors the protection of the bear and its habitat. We can support sound wildlife management research and practices that affect the bear and its future. We can get involved with our politicians in the decision-making process that determines what happens on public lands. We can learn more about habitat and seclusion needs of the big bear and let our elected officials know we support big bear management as opposed to mining, too much timber cutting, road building and other development.

Most importantly, we must make sure our own attitudes are conducive to the conservation of big bears. Our first goal must be to preserve grizzly, brown and polar bears in their natural habitat. To have huntable populations is a bonus. Hunting is secondary to conservation, and with any species it is irresponsible to hunt at the expense of over-kill.

With support from citizens, good wildlife management and some luck, future generations of North Americans will know the sport of hunting big bears, animals that can put excitement into a hunt as no other North American game animal can. No hunter now or in the future should miss out on that opportunity.

BIG BEAR RESOURCES

North American Hunting Club
Member Services Department
P.O. Box 3401
Minnetonka, MN 55343
(800) 922-4868
www.huntingclub.com

Wildlife Forever
10365 W 70th St
Eden Prairie, MN 55334
(952) 833-1522
www.wildlifeforever.org

RECORD-KEEPING ORGANIZATIONS

Boone and Crockett Club
250 Station Drive
Missoula, MT 59801
(406) 542-1888
www.boone-crockett.org

The Longhunter
P.O. Box 67
Friendship, IN 47021
(812) 667-5131
www.nmlra.org

Pope and Young Club
P.O. Box 548
Chatfield, MN 55923
(507) 867-4144
www.pope-young.org

Safari Club International
4800 West Gates Pass Road
Tucson, AZ 85745
(888) 724-HUNT, (602) 620-1220
www.safariclub.org

FISH & GAME DEPARTMENTS

Alaska Department of Fish & Game
P.O. Box 25526
Juneau, AK 99802-5526
(907) 465-4190
www.state.ak.us/adfg

British Columbia Ministry of the Environment,
  Lands & Parks
P.O. Box 9359 Wildlife Branch
Stn Provincial Gov
Victoria, BC V8W 9M2
(250) 387-3205
www.env.gov.bc.ca

Yukon Renewable Resources
Fish & Wildlife Branch
P.O. Box 2703
Whitehorse, YK Y1A 2C6
(867) 667-5221
www.gov.yk.ca/

Northwest Territories Resources,
Wildlife & Economic Development
P.O. Box 28
Tuktoyaktuk, NT X0E 1C0
(867) 977-2350

Alberta Fisheries & Wildlife
  Management Division
Main Flr South Tower Petroleum Plaza
9915 108th St
Edmonton, AB T5K2G8
(780) 427-5185
www.env.gov.ab.ca/

Nunavut
As of this printing, the
Canadian province of Nunavut
does not yet have a structured
wildlife agency. You can get up-
to-date information in the
NAHC Hunting Resource
Directory available
through the NAHC
Member Services
Department.

RIFLE MANUFACTURERS

Browning
One Browning Place
Morgan, UT 84050
(801) 876-2711
www.browning.com

Weatherby Inc.
3100 El Camino Real
Atascadero, CA 93422
(805) 466-1767
www.weatherby.com

Remington Arms Co., Inc.
870 Remington Drive
Madison, NC 27025
(800) 243-9700
www.remington.com

Winchester Firearms
U.S. Repeating Arms Co., Inc.
275 Winchester Avenue
Morgan, UT 84050
(801) 876-3440
www.winchester-guns.com

INDEX